Contents

Contents

Part 1

Introduction

The life of Robert Burns (1759–96)

Robert Burns, the eldest son of a tenant farmer in Ayrshire, Scotland, grew up to a life of hard physical toil, poverty, and acute awareness of social inequality. It was to find 'some kind of counterpoise' to a harsh set of circumstances, and to amuse himself, that he began to write poetry. He passionately wanted to give expression to his ideas and feelings, even if he could not improve his economic lot. By his mid-twenties, although unknown beyond his own district of south-western Scotland, not only had he read widely in both Scots and English, but as an original poet, he had also acquired exceptional mastery of different kinds of poetry in Lowland Scots, including satire. He had become, furthermore, a fluent and accomplished writer of song lyrics. When his father died in 1784, he and his brother rented the farm of Mossgiel, near the village of Mauchline, where he was already well known locally to his peer group for his ready wit and many love affairs.

Burns's nature craved direct communication with his fellow beings and it was around this time that his life as a poet, lover of women, and sardonic commentator on social affairs entered a new, highly active phase. It was as if his father's death had acted as a trigger, releasing a flood of creative energy which demanded expression. He was now 'Rob Mossgiel', farmer and personality in his own right, and his temperament made him intensely ambitious. He took to writing poems on the amusing side of life in the community, and sent 'verse epistles' or letter-poems to other poets of the district, men like John Lapraik from Muirkirk, one of whose compositions Burns chanced to hear one evening at a 'rocking' or social gathering, and David Sillar, a friend and former neighbour whose skill as a fiddler Burns admired.

There were songs to tease the girls of Mauchline, daring satires on church affairs to amuse the bold and free spirits of the community, and deftly controlled socially descriptive poems like 'The Twa Dogs. A Tale' which were, among other things, a safety-valve to help the poet get rid of the intense resentment he sometimes felt at the unequal distribution of wealth in society. 'I now began to be known in the neighbourhood as a maker of rhymes', he wrote. Circulating in manuscript, some of Burns's poems won him a reputation for originality and cleverness, although inevitably his aptitude for hard-hitting personal satire also created one or two enemies in Mauchline and the surrounding district. 'Holy Willie's Prayer' is a prime example of his satirical verse.

In addition to the psychological liberation which his father's death had brought about, there was a more specifically literary stimulus motivating Burns at this period. He owed much to a recent forerunner in Scottish poetry, Robert Fergusson (1750–74). 'Rhyme', he later explained, 'except some religious pieces which are in print, I had given up; but meeting with Fergusson's Scotch Poems, I strung my wildly-sounding rustic lyre with emulating vigour.' The edition of Fergusson's poems which he used was published in 1782 and Burns made what was for him the vital discovery of the work of his fellow Scots poet – 'my elder brother in the Muse' – precisely when its effect was most beneficial.

Seldom can the poems of one individual have had such a salutary influence as a model on the poetic practice of another. There was no question of Burns being in any way inhibited by the achievement of his predecessor, any more than by the poems of Pope, Burns's outstanding eighteenth-century predecessor in sharply satirical English poetry. Instead, in poem after poem he built on the excellence of the past, in this way carrying forward and widening the range of outstanding original work both in Scots and in English.

Burns's personal circumstances always strongly affected his writing. This was very much the case during 1785–6, which was in every way an astonishingly busy year. By the spring of 1786 he had decided to have his poems set up in 'guid black prent' by John Wilson, a Kilmarnock printer, and published by subscription. In the event, *Poems, Chiefly in the Scottish Dialect* appeared in an edition of 612 copies in late July. Arguably, he would not have taken this all-important step but for the scrapes into which he had got himself. At any rate, he now no longer had to contemplate turning his back on Scotland and emigrating to the West Indies, as he had done for some months in the summer of 1786.

He had fallen in love with and made pregnant a girl called Jean Armour, the daughter of a mason in Mauchline. It was not the first time Burns had got a girl into trouble, nor would it be the last; but on this occasion he remained emotionally committed, as did Jean. The couple obtained a simple signed document which in their own eyes was evidence of marriage. Unfortunately, Jean's parents took a very different view. James Armour had a fainting fit, then sent his daughter to Paisley, where he and his wife hoped – vainly, as things turned out – that she might take up again with a more respectable suitor than the erratic poet-farmer of Mossgiel. For his part, Burns reacted by plunging for a time into 'all kinds of dissipation and riot'. At the very time when his *Poems* were creating excitement in Ayrshire and being passed eagerly from hand to hand, Burns felt himself being hounded by hostile legal representatives and members of the Church who disapproved of his morals and strong opinions.

Burns had already given up his share of Mossgiel to his brother Gilbert, and was intent, somewhat desperately, on sailing to Jamaica. The next turn of events is best told in his own words.

> I had taken the last farewell of my few friends; my chest was on the road to Greenock; I had composed my last song I should ever measure in Caledonia, 'The gloomy night is gathering fast', when a letter from Dr Blacklock to a friend of mine overthrew all my schemes by rousing my poetic ambition.

Seldom can any young poet have received encouragement on first publication with more intense feelings of relief than the overwrought Burns. Thomas Blacklock was a blind fellow poet and Ayrshireman, prepared to exert himself on Burns's behalf. Soon, Burns's work was being read by other influential men of letters in Edinburgh, including a network of men from his own region, the south-west of Scotland, and a number of prominent Edinburgh citizens who showed Burns much kindness. The admiration his work aroused was genuine; and along with it went considerable excitement, as he seemed to those who came into contact with him to conform remarkably to an idea which was fashionable at the time, that of a poet of genius springing forth from a 'primitive' background and owing nothing to learning.

In fact, Burns was a voracious reader. He was adroit enough, though, to do nothing obvious now to destroy an image which had helped to create a particular kind of reputation for him in Edinburgh society. An observer later commented shrewdly,

> It was, I know, a part of the machinery, as he called it, of his poetical character to pass for an illiterate ploughman who wrote from pure inspiration.

One early review, in the *Lounger* in December 1786 by Henry Mackenzie – author of the sentimental novel, *The Man of Feeling*, which Burns admired 'next to the Bible' – was especially influential. Mackenzie applied to Burns the words 'this Heaven-taught ploughman'. Before long, the phrase was being repeated in tributes which began to appear in other journals, including a number of London publications.

Thus before the year was out Burns was well and truly launched on the way to literary fame. To his credit, he kept his head and his sense of humour amid all the glare of publicity. Characteristically, at the height of his success he remembered the unhappy fate of Robert Fergusson, whose poems had helped to inspire his own, and was instrumental in having a tombstone erected in Fergusson's honour in the graveyard of the Canongate Church in Edinburgh. Some impression of the poet's appearance and decisive personality can be gleaned from the comments of people who met him in the capital. One noted that

> His dress was plain, but genteel, like that of a farmer of the better sort
> ... His behaviour was suitable to his appearance: neither awkward,
> arrogant, nor affected, but decent, dignified, and simple.

The purpose for which Burns had come to Edinburgh was fulfilled in April
1787 when a second, much enlarged edition of his *Poems* was published
thanks to leading members of the Caledonian Hunt, an influential associa-
tion of nobility and gentry. Technically speaking, Burns was responsible
once again for publishing the new edition, but after taking advice he had
sold the copyright of his poems to William Creech, an Edinburgh book-
seller. After all his years of hardship and isolation, it is not surprising that
Burns was determined to make the most of the chance created by his
modest literary earnings to take a prolonged break from farming and see
something of life beyond Ayrshire. Thus, when his *Poems* were once more
in print, he set off on a tour in the Borders. Two visits to the Highlands and
one to Central Scotland were to follow later in the year. He was now a
celebrated national figure.

His stated idea in travelling had to do with his aesthetic and patriotic
feelings. Just as, when living in Ayrshire, he had felt a strong wish to
respond to the beauty of the region, and to its history, so now he was
drawn to widen his experience, with the possibility of becoming Scot-
land's leading poet, 'Caledonia's bard'. A letter to Mrs Dunlop of Dunlop
of 22 March 1787 is explicit in describing his motives:

> I have no greater, no dearer aim than to have it in my power, unplagu'd
> with the routine of business, for which Heaven knows I am unfit
> enough, to make leisurely pilgrimages through Caledonia; to sit on the
> fields of her battles; to wander on the romantic banks of her rivers; and
> to muse by the stately tower of venerable ruins, once the honored
> abodes of her heroes.

Interestingly, his immediate written accounts of his journeyings in
Scotland – in the form of journals and letters – offer a rather different
image of Burns on tour, at once more down-to-earth and less systematic in
his approach. He jots down brief notes on the appearance of crops – rather
than of landscapes – and assesses the character of the local farmers and the
beauty of young women, instead of commenting in any detail on cultural
history.

Burns's travelling companion in the Borders was an Edinburgh law
student called Bob Ainslie, whose family came from the Dunbar area.
They naturally spent a fair amount of time in the eastern part of the
extensive Border country, crossing briefly into England for the first and
last time in Burns's life. (On the way to Carlisle, the poet had 'a strange
romantic adventure' with a girl who offered to take him 'for a Gretna-
green affair' or elopement. Burns's response did not include marriage;

therefore 'finding herself un peu trompée in her man, she sheers off'.) Yet Burns did in fact live up to his own aspirations as conveyed to Mrs Dunlop, but in ways which perhaps he had not fully anticipated before setting out on the road. A number of poems and songs were written straightaway; and more important, Burns laid in a store of vivid firsthand experiences of places, persons, and melodies. Especially as a songwriter, he was to draw on the impressions and memories collected on this tour for the rest of his life.

Indeed, both in Edinburgh and on travels through Scotland which his literary success made possible, Burns met individuals who shared his enthusiasm for traditional Scottish songs and melodies. Since early in the century there had been a movement afoot – at first little more than a fitful and sporadic scholarly pursuit, but later a more widespread phenomenon, involving people from different classes and backgrounds – to bring together whatever from the past seemed to express Scotland's national identity, including part of the country's rich heritage of poetry, music and song.

Antiquarianism of this patriotic type had been given fresh energy and direction in Burns's day by current ideas about the value of intellectual enquiry, working upon what many Scots felt to be a loss of national pride and identity caused by the Union of Parliaments in 1707. Mind and heart were both involved, and it was this which appealed to Burns. For many years he had been attracted by the idea of gathering some of the old songs current in Ayrshire, and supplying words where need be to accompany the surviving old melodies. In a notebook he wrote,

> There is a degree of wild irregularity in many of the compositions & Fragments which are daily sung ... by my compeers, the common people ... This has made me sometimes imagine that perhaps, it might be possible for a Scotch Poet, with a nice, judicious ear, to set compositions to many of our most favorite airs.

Accordingly, when he met an unassuming music engraver called James Johnson in the spring of 1787 at an Edinburgh tavern gathering of a convivial society, and heard about Johnson's plan to collect and edit all the surviving songs of Scotland, he was immediately interested, and promised to do what he could to assist. Instinctively, he recognised that his artistic future lay in writing and editing the songs of the people, rather than working to please literary critics who wanted him to write long poems, preferably in English.

Burns spent a second winter in Edinburgh. Eventually in 1788, he returned somewhat reluctantly to tenant farming in south-west Scotland, having now married Jean Armour. For a time he combined farming with work in the Excise, because the latter was salaried and he had a growing young family; then he became a full-time Excise officer in Dumfries. His most famous poem, 'Tam o' Shanter', was written in 1790, but for the most part he devoted the leisure hours of his later years to the writing and collecting of Scottish songs, in which he was passionately interested. From 1788 until his death in July 1796 he was the principal contributor to and virtual editor of the greatest of all Scottish song collections, Johnson's *Scots Musical Museum* (6 volumes, 1787–1803). He also supplied the words of many songs for George Thomson's *Select Collection of Original Scotish Airs* (5 volumes, 1793–1818), which boasted among its musical contributors Haydn and Beethoven. In all, he wrote more than three hundred songs.

Partly because of the sensational appeal of some aspects of Burns's life, his varied art and craftmanship as a writer still tend to remain neglected after two hundred years. While there is a sense in which it can be argued that he failed to follow up the success of his first collection of poems with further orthodox literary work in the form of books, Burns was capable of brilliance in poetic phrasing to the end of his life, and he was consistently prolific as a songwriter of the highest quality.

Language

At first glance, the language of Burns's poetry is likely to strike many readers as difficult and foreign. Intrinsically, however, it can be understood at least as readily as Chaucer's English by anyone willing to spend a little time on Scots words, their meaning, and how they sound when read aloud. Historically, English and Lowland Scots are both derived from the same original language, Anglo-Saxon, though Scots has a Norse element and some Dutch, French, and Gaelic not shared with English, which in turn contains significant borrowings and linguistic forms of its own.

The first requirement is to read for sense, and then for sound, or the converse – enjoying the 'music' of the words. Reading Burns's poems and songs may at first seem difficult for two reasons. These are the fact that he lived two hundred years ago, and that he wrote much of his best work not in English, but in Scots. It is perfectly possible, however, for any open-minded student to come to understand his writings. Focus on the meaning of any particular poem. Read the text, and find out the broad meaning of the whole, then of particular unfamiliar words and phrases. You can do this by consulting your edition of the poetry, and also this book.

It probably helped Burns in his discovery over the years of the varied possibilities open to a poet using Scots that while his mother was an Ayrshire woman, with a stock of songs and proverbial sayings, his father was an incomer from another well-endowed linguistic area, the north-east of Scotland; and one moreover who insisted that his family acquire skills in the reading and writing of English. Burns is completely at home in his native tongue, enriching the spoken dialect of Ayrshire with a judicious selection of words drawn from his reading of earlier Scottish poetry. 'The Holy Fair', for example, uses plain direct Scots to turn simple and natural conversation into poetry:

Upon a simmer Sunday morn,	summer
When Nature's face is fair,	
I walked forth to view the corn,	
An' snuff the callor air.	sniff, fresh
The rising sun, owre GALSTON Muirs,	over
Wi' glorious light was glintan;	
The hares were hirplan down the furrs,	scampering, furrows
The lav'rocks they were chantan	larks
Fu' sweet that day.	

Burns has evoked a summer morning clearly and with feeling, so as to put the reader in the right mood for the appearance a little later of Fun, his companion for the day. Rhythm helps to imbue the passage with its cheerful mood, tone, and feeling. It was the poet's custom to give clues to tone and mood in this way.

The many clues to meaning which Burns supplies help the reader to understand his poems and songs without too much difficulty, even granted that it is necessary to look up the meaning of unfamiliar Scots words in his poetry. The overall sense of what he writes is seldom in doubt. Here, for instance, he writes that it is a 'glorious' or lovely day. It is easy to grasp that 'simmer' is a Scots way of pronouncing summer. We can also grasp without difficulty that the poet is a country-dweller, since he goes out to view the corn, and sees hares. For every difficult word, such as callor, hirplan, lav'rocks, there are several words in English or 'Scots English' such as 'snuff' (sniff).

In much the same way, he establishes that the smiling figure of FUN is to be thought of positively, as congenial and light-hearted, in complete contrast to the long-faced SUPERSTITION and HYPOCRISY. She takes the poet's hand, and invites him to join her in mocking the other two, 'that runkl'd pair'. The context shows that 'runkl'd' is simply the Scots form of 'wrinkled', and conveys instinctive fellow-feeling between the poet and FUN. He replies immediately to the effect that he will put on his best clothes, and that FUN and he will enjoy commenting on the others who are present at Mauchline Fair. The clear implication is that SUPERSTITION and HYPOCRISY will be their main targets. Once again, the poem successfully identifies a key idea through rhythm, tone and mood. By paying attention to the context, the reader can quickly assimilate the leading ideas being put forward.

Burns's songs can be understood in much the same way. The tunes impart an extra dimension of tone and mood, often establishing exactly how the words are intended, but more often than not the latter alone convey the feeling of the song clearly. For example, it can readily be seen – as well as heard – that the mood of 'Ae fond kiss, and then we sever' is bitter-sweet. The first line conveys as much. Likewise, the approach adopted in 'It was upon a Lammas night' is unmistakably jaunty and confident, even without the original melody, which matches the poet's happy spirit. In a third example, 'Mary Morison', the mood is wistful rather than assured. This is a song of longing, in which the writer expresses intense admiration for Mary, rather than triumph. In each song, thought and feeling belong together in a single unity.

A note on the text

Burns wrote freely and fluently. From time to time he would send to individuals he liked or admired handwritten versions of published or unpublished poems or songs he thought they might like to receive from him. His first collection of poetry was published at Kilmarnock in 1786. The following year he brought out an enlarged edition in Edinburgh, with the same title, *Poems, Chiefly in the Scottish Dialect*. One clear sign that he succeeded in public estimation can be seen in the fact that, within a few weeks of its publication in April 1787, he was offered the freedom of no fewer than three Scottish towns: Jedburgh, Dumfries, and Dumbarton.

After the success of 1787, Burns continued to write poems, but increasingly often his best work was in songwriting. Yet while remaining the chief contributor to *The Scots Musical Museum* and to *A Select Collection of Original Scottish Airs*, Burns during this time also planned and published a new edition of his poems, issued by Creech in Edinburgh in 1793. 'Tam o' Shanter' first appeared in a book as a footnote in the second volume of Burns's friend Francis Grose's *Antiquities of Scotland*, 1791.

Successful as a poet, and a writer and collector of songs, he never grew rich on his writing, and died struggling with debts.

This book is largely based on poems and songs included in *Robert Burns: Poems in Scots and English* (ed. Donald Low), Everyman Paperbacks, 1993. Libraries may have the same editor's *The Songs of Robert Burns*, Routledge, 1993, which includes the following songs discussed below:

'Mary Morison'
'The rantin dog the Daddie o't'
'[There was a lad]'
'Afton Water'
'Tam Glen'
'Ay waukin O'
'A red red Rose'
'Auld lang syne'

Note that not all of these songs are labelled with a 'title'. Songs without a title are referred to by the first line.

These songs, and also 'Death and Doctor Hornbook', are included in *The Poems and Songs of Robert Burns* (ed. James Kinsley), Oxford University Press, 3 vols, 1968, 1 vol edition without notes, 1969.

Robert Burns: Selected Poems (ed. Carol McGuirk), Penguin, 1993, includes 'Death and Doctor Hornbook' and several of the songs discussed in this book.

Part 2

Summaries

Poems

'The Twa Dogs. A Tale'

This poem presents an imaginary conversation between two dogs – Caesar, whose owner is a rich man, and Luath, who belongs to a poor man. The dogs describe sharply contrasting ways of life, noting both surprising contentment among the poor and lack of real happiness among their social superiors. The friendship between animals implies a rebuke to unkind or snobbish humans.

COMMENTARY:

Burns shows Caesar, the rich man's Newfoundland, kept as a pet, to be no spoiled creature with his nose in the air, but instead a ready companion for the 'gash an' faithfu' tyke' Luath, keen to share with him their common interests as dogs, and to talk, on equal terms. The poem works by setting up Luath's enthusiastic praise for poor people beside Caesar's sharp criticism of the wealthy. Not only is the freedom from pretension on the part of animals a refreshing contrast to human divisiveness, but Caesar's genial outlook wins the goodwill of the reader: he is an honest observer of rich people's lives, one who can be trusted.

NOTES AND GLOSSARY:

thrang:	busy
lugs:	ears
whalpet:	whelped
brew:	splendid, fine
fient a:	not a bit of
messan:	mongrel
Kirk:	church
Smiddie:	smithy, blacksmith
tawted:	matted
tyke:	cur
duddie:	ragged
wad:	would have
stan't:	stood

stroan't:	watered
stanes:	stones
billie:	fellow
lang syne:	long ago
gash:	wise
lap:	leapt
sheugh:	ditch
dyke:	stone wall
sonsie:	pleasant
baws'nt:	white-striped
ilka:	every
towzie:	shaggy
gawsie:	cheerful
hurdies:	buttocks
fain o':	fond of
unco pack:	very intimate
thegither:	together
whyles:	at times
snuff'd:	sniffed
snowket:	poked about
modewurks:	moles
howket:	dug
scour'd:	ranged
wi' mony a farce:	with many a joke
bodies:	folk
ava:	at all
kane:	payment in kind
stents:	dues
steeks:	stitches
Geordie **keeks:**	guinea peeps
een:	evening
steghan:	cramming
ha' folk:	servants
peghan:	stomach
trashtrie:	rubbish
wastrie:	waste
Whipper-in:	hunt-servant
wonner:	wonder
Cot-folk:	cottagers
painch:	paunch
Trowth:	indeed
fash't:	troubled
Cotter howkan:	a farmworker digging
biggan:	building

Bairan:	clearing
smytrie:	swarm
duddie weans:	dirty children
han'-daurk:	physical work
thack an' raep:	thatch and rope
sair:	sore
maun:	must
buirdly chiels:	well-built lads
hizzies:	wenches
huff'd:	scolded
brock:	badger
court-day:	rent-day
wae:	sad
thole:	endure
snash:	insolence
poind:	distrain, seize
's ane wad:	as one would
poortith:	poverty
grushie:	thriving
weans:	children
twalpennie:	twelvepence
nappy:	ale
bodies:	folk
ferlie:	marvel
rantan:	romping
Kirns:	harvest-homes
reeks:	smokes
ream:	foam
luntan:	smoking
sneeshin mill:	snuff-box
cantie:	lively
crackan crouse:	talking cheerfully
fain:	glad
owre:	often
fawsont:	respectable
riven:	torn
aiblins:	perhaps
saul indentin:	soul pledging
Haith:	a petty oath
gaun:	going
waft:	sea trip
tak a whirl:	go on the Grand Tour
rives:	splits
entails:	estate succession

rout:	road
fecht wi' nowt:	fight cattle
bowses:	drinks
drumlie:	cloudy
ga's:	galls
b-res:	cracks
ch-ncres:	ulcers
gate:	way
foughten:	worn out
gear:	wealth
thae:	these
Fient haet:	not one
timmer:	timber
Limmer:	mistress
ne'er-a-bit:	not in the least
steer:	affect
fear:	frighten
gentles:	great folks
sair-wark:	hard work
banes:	bones
grips an' granes:	gripes and groans
enow:	enough
sturt:	trouble
pleugh:	plough
dizzen:	dozen cuts of yarn
warst:	worst of all
want o' wark:	sheer lack of work
deil-haet:	damn-all
cast out:	fall out
party-matches:	card-contests
sowther:	patch up
wh-ring:	whoring
Niest:	next
a':	all
run deils:	complete devils
an' jads:	and hussies
lee-lang:	live-long
crabbet leuks:	cross looks
devil's *pictur'd beuks*:	playing cards
gloamin:	twilight
bum-clock:	beetle
kye:	cattle
rowtan:	lowing
loan:	pasture

'Scotch Drink'

A poem which praises whisky as Scotland's national drink. While others have written of foreign drinks like wine, whisky delights the poet, who goes on to illustrate some of the many ways in which, he claims, it offers vital social benefits. According to Burns, too, he owes many rhymes to the inspiring effect of a dram. Short of money he may be, but this will not get the better of him as long as he has life's essentials, which include a whisky gill and abundance of rhyme.

COMMENTARY:
Burns writes in unqualified praise of the merits of whisky. No hint is given of any risk of the abuse of alcohol: instead the reader finds a varied and detailed celebration of how Scotland's native drink, made from barley, confers advantages. Whisky cheers careworn hearts and revives the weary. Above all, it gives pleasure, whether in public or private life, at the time of harvest or on New Year morning. Scotch drink makes for virility and also helps to end quarrels. In that sense its presence is of practical value:

> It's aye the cheapest Lawyer's fee
>> To taste the barrel.

The poet will hear nothing in praise of such foreign drinks as wine or brandy. Instead, he expresses his gratitude as poet for the fact that whisky gives energy to his verses, and deplores recent government action which has ended the exemption from tax of Ferintosh, a well-known brand. The second last verse refers with contempt to 'leeches of the Excise'. This is ironic, as Burns was later to work as an exciseman himself.

Imagery and language are deliberately chosen to add strength to a poem celebrating Scotland's own native alcoholic spirit, whisky. Brandy and wine are mentioned only to be dismissed with contempt. In verse after verse, the poet's manner expresses his attitude of uncompromising praise for whisky at the expense of such allegedly inferior foreign drinks. He appeals to his fellow-Scots by making use of Scots vernacular phrases with which they alone are likely to be familiar. The structure of the poem is that of a secular hymn of praise, with many verses of direct address lending an air of enthusiastic enjoyment. Ironically, the poet refers to whisky as his muse, traditionally a goddess invoked to inspire poetry.

NOTES AND GLOSSARY:

druken:	drunken
Bacchus:	the god of wine
crabbed:	cross
grate:	sound harshly
lug:	ear

Scotch bear:	barley
guid:	good
auld:	old
wimplin:	twisting
jink:	slip fast
ream:	froth
faem:	foam
haughs:	level land by river
Aits:	oats
awnie:	bearded
een:	evening
Leeze me on thee:	you delight me
John Barleycorn:	whisky
chows her cood:	chews her cud
souple:	supple
wale:	choice
kail:	vegetable broth
wame:	stomach
scrievin:	gliding swiftly
doited:	stupefied
Lear:	learning
sair:	hard
siller:	silver
weed:	dress
pirratch:	porridge
kitchens:	seasons
rants:	sprees
saunts:	saints, 'the elect'
tents:	field pulpits
reams:	froths
reekan:	smoking
cog or bicker:	wooden drinking cups
spir'tual burn:	water used in brewing
gusty sucker:	tasty sugar
gies:	gives
graith:	ploughing gear
freath:	froth
lugget caup:	wooden dish with handles
Burnewin:	blacksmith
chap:	stroke
Nae:	no
airn:	iron
brawnie:	strong
banie:	bony, big-boned

chiel:	fellow
owrehip:	over the hip
forehammer:	sledge-hammer
studdie:	anvil
dinsome:	noisy
skirlin weanies:	yelling infants
coofs:	clowns
Wae worth:	cursed be
tight:	virile
neebors:	neighbours
wud:	angry
barley-brie:	whisky
wyte:	blame
monie:	many
weet their weason:	wet their throat
spier:	ask
Wae:	woe
burnan:	burning
Fell:	severe
brash:	illness
Twins:	deprives
doylt:	muddled
druken hash:	drunken waster
warst faes:	worst foes
plackless:	penniless
dearthfu':	costly
mell:	meddle
Gravels:	urinary pains
blather:	bladder
gruntle:	snout
glunch:	frown
owre:	over
Bardie's:	poet's
cranks:	noises
Ferintosh:	a whisky
hoast:	cough
Thae:	those
stells:	stills
Haud:	hold
Deil:	devil
ance:	once
blinkers:	spies, cheats
brunstane:	brimstone
Hale breeks:	intact breeches

rowth:	abundance
Tak:	take

'The Holy Fair'

A poem which turns on contrasts between the profession of virtue and serious aims at a country communion, and actual human inclinations. Burns meets three female figures on a summer Sunday, heading for a religious festival. Unlike Superstition and Hypocrisy, who want none of his company, Fun welcomes him and is ready to share the day's amusement with him at the expense of the other two. In keeping with this opening, the holy fair brings together markedly different groups. On the one hand are devotees of religious orthodoxy, including the sanctimonious, and preachers of both a hellfire-and-brimstone stamp and a coldly moralistic type. In contrast to these are the many people who are primarily interested in enjoying themselves.

COMMENTARY:
The 9-line verse-form has a long history in Scots as a means of describing social events which bring people together for some communal event or purpose. Burns uses it deftly, and straightaway succeeds in conveying a sense of anticipation on a lovely day. His meeting with two gloomy figures and with Fun, a very different, cheerful young woman, signals that the description of events to follow will include a good deal of pointed social satire. Groups of stanzas, as well as brief individual portraits, build up a picture of participants with entirely different aims and attitudes. There is much talk of religion, some of it uncompromisingly severe and some lukewarm; but the attention of those who have come together, ostensibly only to worship, keeps shifting to less exalted themes. Cumulatively, the poem establishes that superstition, hypocrisy, and fun are indeed all present and influential in the society which is described. Burns holds up to scorn the life-denying outlook of 'the Elect', who have 'screw'd-up, grace-proud faces'. His sympathies are with those who indulge in laughter, drink, and sex. There is an implication that these are activities to be welcomed as belonging to nature, like the summer sunshine which opens the poem. The language of the poem is cheerful and direct, but also reflects the hypocritical striking of attitudes by those who wish to be considered holy. Burns's imagery is robust and explicit.

NOTES AND GLOSSARY:

simmer:	summer
snuff:	sniff
callor:	fresh
hirplan:	moving unevenly forwards

furrs:	furrows
lav'rocks:	larks
Fu':	very
glowr'd:	gazed intently
hizzies:	wenches
skelpan:	hurrying
manteeles:	capes
ane:	one
lyart:	grey
gaed:	went
a wee a-back:	a little behind
twa:	two
claes:	clothes
lang:	long
slaes:	sloes
cam:	came
hap-step-an'-loup:	hop-step-and-jump
lambie:	little lamb
curchie:	curtsy
ken:	know
bonie:	attractive
canna:	cannot
spak:	spoke
hae gien the feck:	have given most
comman's:	commandments
screed:	rent, tear
gaun:	going
******** holy fair:	[Mauchline] holy fair
daffin:	frolic
Gin:	if
yon runkl'd:	that wrinkled
sark:	shirt
we'se hae:	we will have
hame:	home
crowdie-time:	breakfast-time
gash:	smart
graith:	habit
hoddan:	jogging
cotters:	cottagers
swankies:	strapping lads
braid-claith:	broad-cloth
skelpan:	hurrying
barefit:	barefoot
thrang:	busy, in a crowd

monie a whang:	many a thick slice
farls:	bits of oaten bannock
crump:	hard and brittle
tippence:	twopence
dails:	deal planks
bleth'ran:	chatting
twathree-wh-res:	two or three whores
tittlan jads:	gossiping hussies
Wabster:	weaver
Blackguarding:	roistering
K*****ck:**	Kilmarnock
claes:	clothes
fyl'd:	dirtied
Anither:	another
swatch:	sample
screw'd up:	sanctimonious
Thrang:	throng
ain:	own
clinkan:	sitting smartly
loof:	palm
Unkend:	unknown
****** speels:**	[Moodie] climbs
s-lv-t--n:	salvation
Hornie:	Satan
'Mang:	among
*******'s:	[Hornie][Satan]'s
vera:	very
het hame:	hot home (Hell)
eldritch:	hideous
cantharidian:	sexually stimulating
plaisters:	plasters
tent:	field pulpit
***** opens:**	[Smith] opens
cauld:	cold
aff:	off
guid:	good
sic poosion'd nostrum: such a poisoned remedy	
For *****:**	for [Peebles]
water-fit:	river-mouth
mim:	demure
Wee ****:**	Wee [Miller]
niest:	next
raibles:	gabbles
weel:	well

birkie:	fellow
cannilie he hums them:	dextrously he takes them in
hafflins-wise:	in half measure
butt an' ben:	in outer and inner room
yill-caup:	ale-cup
bakes an' gills:	biscuits and drams
-stowp:	measure
Leeze me on:	I'm all for
waukens Lear:	wakens learning
pangs:	stuffs
fou:	full
penny-wheep:	small beer
kittle:	rouse
saul:	soul
steer:	stir
toddy:	whisky, hot water and sugar
leuk:	expression
neuk:	corner
L — 's:	Lord's
touts:	blasts
rairan:	roaring
****** . . . spairan:	Russel . . . sparing
H-ll:	Hell
vera:	very
lowan brunstane:	blazing brimstone
Wad:	would
whun-stane:	whinstone
neebor *snoran*:	neighbour snoring
owre:	over
crouded:	crowded
yill:	ale
cogs an' caups:	dishes and bowls
furms:	forms
dawds:	hunks
gawsie, gash *Guidwife*:	jovial, neat matron
Syne:	then
kebbuk:	cheese
Guidmen:	husbands
Waesucks:	alas
melvie his braw claithing!:	soil his attractive clothing
dinna:	do not
kebbuck-heel:	heel of cheese
Clinkumbell:	bellringer
rattlan tow:	rattling rope

jow an' croon:	toll and sound
dow:	are able
slaps:	gaps in the dyke
billies:	fellows
shoon:	shoes
crack:	chat
stane:	stone
gin night are gane:	by nightfall are gone
saft:	soft
jobs:	intrigues
Houghmagandie:	fornication

'Address to the Deil'

A playful address to the Devil, called in the first verse names which range from Satan to the familiar Scots forms Auld Hornie and Clootie. Burns cites many contrasting examples of the Devil's alleged power over mortals. These relate to folklore and superstitious awe. Burns shows that people have been brought up to believe in the Devil as the source and cause of quite different kinds of misfortune. The overall effect of the poem is to amuse and reduce fear.

COMMENTARY:

A quotation from *Paradise Lost* introduces the poem, which suggests a grave treatment of its subject. Burns's way of addressing the Devil, however, is mocking and disrespectful. 'Address to the Deil' raises searching questions about a good many attitudes taken for granted in Burns's time. 'I've heard my rev'rend *Graunie* say' points to the poet's subtle humour. The language is homely and irreverent, and by its very familiarity implies that solemn notions about the Devil are out of date. As the poem develops, it becomes clear that Burns's purpose is to satirise as lacking in reason the habit of accepting without question conventional ideas about Satan's involvement in much that is attributed to his agency. The speaker up to line 84 is a naive and credulous countryman. Then in the final seven stanzas the poet writes pointedly about the condemnation of love affairs conveyed by traditional views of a punitive God.

NOTES AND GLOSSARY:

Clootie:	cloven-hoof
Spairges:	bespatters
brunstane cootie:	brimstone tub
scaud:	scald
Hangie:	Hangman
deil:	devil

skelp:	smack
lowan heugh:	blazing pit
lag:	backward
blate:	bashful
scaur:	afraid
Tirlan the *kirks*:	uncovering the churches
Graunie:	grandmother
lanely:	lonely
eldritch croon:	unearthly moan
douse:	sober
'yont the dyke:	beyond the stone wall
bumman:	humming
boortries:	elder trees
sklentan:	slanting
Ayont the lough:	beyond the loch
rash-buss:	clump of rushes
sugh:	sound of wind
neive:	fist
stoor:	harsh
squatter'd:	flew in water
muirs:	moors
howcket:	exhumed
kirn:	churn
dawtet:	spoiled
twal-pint:	twelve-pint
yell's:	milkless as
Bill:	bull
-Guidmen:	-husbands
croose:	confident
wark-lume:	work-loom
cantraip:	magic
bit:	critical moment
thowes:	thaws
snawy hoord:	snowy drift
jinglan:	cracking
boord:	surface
kelpies:	-horse demons
Spunkies:	wills o' the wisp
bleezan:	blazing
Aff straught:	off straight
Lang syne:	long ago
yard:	garden
swaird:	sward
snick-:	latch-

incog:	unknown
brogue:	trick
warld a shog:	world a shock
bizz:	stir
reeket duds:	smoky clothes
reestet gizz:	'cured' wig
smoutie phiz:	ugly face
sklented:	directed aslant
lows'd:	loosed
Scawl:	abusive woman
warst ava:	worst of all
fechtin:	fighting
ding a'*Lallan*:	weary Lowland
***Erse*:**	Gaelic
***Bardie*:**	poet
linkan:	going briskly
jinkan:	side-stepping
an' men':	and mend
aiblins:	perhaps
dinna ken:	don't know
***stake*:**	chance
wae:	unhappy

'Poor Mailie's Elegy'

A mock-elegy for a dead sheep. Burns wrote an earlier comic poem, 'The Death and Dying Words of Poor Mailie', when his only ewe died after being entangled in a rope. 'Poor Mailie's Elegy' refers directly to the rope in line 38 and presents Mailie playfully as a true friend of the poet, a 'sheep o' sense'.

COMMENTARY:
This is the first of many poems written in what was to become Burns's favourite verse-form, the 6-line 'Standart Habbie', named after *The Life and Death of Habbie Simpson*, a seventeenth-century Scots comic elegy by Robert Sempill. The poet pretends to feel accutely for the death of a sheep, praising her as a true friend and companion, and celebrating the quality of her having come from beyond the Tweed. The structure of the poem uses repetition and exaggeration to show that its opening line

> Lament in rhyme, lament in prose

is merely a joke.

Other poems written in the same stanza but for purposes other than comic elegy include 'To J.S****' and 'The Vision'.

NOTES AND GLOSSARY:

saut:	salt
Bardie's:	poet's
a' remead:	all cure
cape-stane:	coping-stone
warl's gear:	worldly property
dowie:	sad
neebor:	neighbour
town:	village, farm
wat:	know
mense:	discretion
brak:	broke
lanely:	lonely
spence:	inner room
howe:	valley
yowe:	ewe
till:	to
knowe:	knoll, or round hillock
rowe:	roll
get:	offspring
tips:	tups
tauted ket:	matted fleece
'yont:	beyond
fleesh:	fleece
clips:	shears
Wae worth:	woe to
wanchancie:	unlucky
raep:	rope
girn an' gape:	twist the features in rage
croon:	moan
aboon:	above

'To J. S****'

This verse 'epistle' or letter belongs to a group of poems addressed by Burns to those cronies or acquaintances with whom he had common interests. James Smith, six years younger than Burns, was one of his best friends in the village of Mauchline. The poem celebrates friendship, and expresses positive ideas relating to Burns's enthusiasm for poetry, and offers reflections on life at large.

COMMENTARY:
That Burns had worn out shoes visiting Smith (twenty pairs, he claims in stanza 2) is proof of the mutual affection and understanding between the

two. One indication is the fact that Burns can tease him for being of small stature; another that he can write with spontaneous freedom about the poetic mood which has him in its thrall, and ask if Smith has a leisure-moment to hear what is coming. The informal language and imagery of

> Just now I've taen the fit o' rhyme,
> My barmie noddle's working prime

help to establish the sociable mood of the poem. A barmie noddle is a yeasty or fermenting brain. Lacking money, but not country wit, he writes poetry for fun, he declares, rather than for other motives. If the book of poems he has chosen to publish fails to bring fame, so be it: he will wander on regardless. Calm respectability is not for him. Life offers magical pleasures, especially in youth, including female companionship. What he asks for above all is plenty of rhymes.

NOTES AND GLOSSARY:

sleest:	cleverest
pawkie:	humorous
rief:	plunder
warlock-breef:	charm/wizard-spell
prief:	proof
aboon:	above
shoon:	shoes
carlin:	old woman
scrimpet:	stunted
barmie noddle:	yeasty brain
yerket:	stirred
neebor:	neighbour
clash:	talk
fash:	bother about
russet coat:	poor man's rural wear
groat:	small coin
in requit:	by way of compensation
taen a sklent:	taken a slant/turn
prent:	print
hoolie:	take leisure, stop
red:	advise
tak tent:	take care
shaw:	show
deep:	well-versed
thrang:	busily
lanely:	lonely
howes:	hollows
tentless:	careless

croud:	crowd
sae:	so far as
fu':	full
speel'd:	climbed
Eild:	Old Age
hostan:	coughing
hirplan:	limping
gloamin:	twilight
swat:	sweated
But:	without
canie:	cautious
cozie:	comfortable
wights:	fellows
Luna:	Moon
Terra:	Earth
rowth:	plenty
dreeping:	dripping
hing:	hang
claes:	clothes
yill:	ale
Cairds:	tinkers
sconner:	feel disgust
Cit:	townsman
hale:	healthy
water-brose:	porridge
muslin-kail:	meatless broth
e'e:	eye
lug:	ear
jouk:	dodge
douse:	sedate
dyke:	stone wall
ferly:	wonder
hairum-scairum:	wild
ram-stam:	reckless
haud:	hold
quat:	end

'The Vision'

The poet describes how he arrives home exhausted at the end of a hard day's work, and wonders whether he is right to have spent so much time and effort writing poetry, when he could have been earning money instead. When he is in this depressed state, however, he is surprised to see an attractive female figure in his cottage. She 'with an elder sister's air' explains that she is Coila, one of a number of guardian spirits responsible for valuable public activities relating to his part of Ayrshire, charged specifically in this instance with helping protect and develop his individual poetic gifts.

COMMENTARY:
Burns here uses for a solemn reflective purpose the verse form first found in 'Poor Mailie's Elegy'. He opens with a vivid description in Scots of arriving home tired and dejected, struck by his own lack of material success because of his habit of writing poetry. The appearance of an unexpected visitor captures his interest. He takes her to be 'some SCOTTISH MUSE', and is impressed both by her beauty and by the fact that her mantle clearly shows specific well-loved rivers and scenes he has written about. Already the poem has made a transition from Scots to English, the language of serious reflection in Lowland Scotland in the eighteenth century. While it is possible to argue that Burns's handling of Coila's long speech in English does not match the sheer energy of the opening description in Scots, the meaning which Burns conveys in the poem requires both. In Duan Second or part two, his guest addresses him in English 'with an elder Sister's air'. She informs him that different spirits are responsible for various human activities, and identifies herself as Coila. After explaining how she has watched over his early efforts as a country poet, including mistakes caused by youthful enthusiasm, she reminds him of values he must continue to support in his role as a rustic Bard, and crowns him with a holly wreath before leaving.

NOTES AND GLOSSARY:

quat:	left
Maukin:	the hare
kail-yards:	kitchen-gardens
snaws:	snows
flingin-tree:	flail
lee-lang day:	all day long
Ben i' the *Spence*:	into the parlour
lanely, by the ingle-cheek:	lonely, by the fireside
reek:	smoke
hoast-provoking smeek:	cough-provoking smoke
auld:	old
biggin:	building
rattons:	rats
riggin:	roof
mottie:	dusty
blethers:	nonsense, idle talk
guid:	good

harket:	listened to
by this:	by now
clarket:	written up
-sarket:	-shirted
coof:	fool
wauket loof:	calloused palm
aith:	oath
snick:	latch
ingle-lowe:	firelight
bleezan:	blazing
tight:	shapely
Hizzie:	wench
whisht:	silence
dusht:	pushed by a ram
ben:	within
scrimply:	scarcely
peer:	equal
straught:	straight
Nane:	none
staw:	stole
Sodger:	soldier
Potosi's mine:	silver, gold and copper mines in S. W. Bolivia

'The Cotter's Saturday Night'

Introduced by a quotation from Gray's *Elegy* which draws attention to the dignity of poor people's lives, the poem supplies a detailed account of the practical social outlook and living concerns of a poor cotter and his family. 'The Cotter's Saturday Night' presents the picture of a family, and focuses in particular on the eldest daughter Jenny, her suitor who visits the household on Saturday night, and their creditable courtship. Burns praises the genuine values upheld by the family's example and worship, noting the difference between true belief and the superficiality of a mere show of religion.

COMMENTARY:

After addressing a friend in the first 9-line stanza of the poem, Burns describes the homecoming of a cotter or cottager at the end of his working week. Saturday night is special in as much as it is the end of the week, a time for the busy family to meet and talk quietly, and the evening before Sunday. Stanza 2 echoes the opening of Gray's 'Elegy Written in a Country Churchyard'. Burns's poem too celebrates the integrity shown by poor people. He makes use of a combination of Scots and English, employing the latter especially to convey serious reflection. While there are toddlers in the household, the cotter's older children are already in service on neighbouring farms. The cotter and his wife are shown as being prepared to make sacrifices for their sons and daughters. Jenny receives special attention both as their first child and because of the romantic interest which attaches to her being courted by a likeable young man. Burns places emphasis on the worship which follows supper, praising Scottish psalm tunes, and states that Scotland's essential grandeur arises from such scenes as the poem describes.

NOTES AND GLOSSARY:

meed:	reward
ween:	believe
blaws:	blows
sugh:	rushing sound
pleugh:	plough
craws:	crows
COTTER:	farm tenant, cottager
moil:	drudgery
Cot:	cottage
stacher:	stagger
flichterin:	fluttering
wee-bit ingle:	little bit of fire
-stane:	-stone
kiaugh:	anxiety
Belyve:	soon
drapping:	dropping
ca!:	drive
tentie rin:	careful run
cannie:	quiet
neebor:	neighbouring
e'e:	eye
braw:	attractive
sair-:	hard-
spiers:	asks
uncos:	news, strange things
Gars auld claes:	makes old clothes
amaist:	almost
eydent:	diligent
jauk:	trifle
convoy:	escort
hafflins:	half
cracks:	talks
kye:	cattle
blate and laithfu':	shy and bashful

lave:	rest
healsome *Porritch*:	wholesome porridge
soupe:	food
Hawkie:	cow
hallan:	partition
chows her cood:	chews her cud
-hain'd kebbuck:	kept cheese
fell:	pungent
towmond:	twelvemonth
Lint:	flax
bell:	bloom
ha'-:	hall-
lyart haffets:	grey temples
wales:	chooses
beets:	adds fuel to

'To a Mouse'

A widely anthologised poem which conveys Burns's tender feeling for a small defenceless animal. He believes that humans have a duty to respect 'Nature's social union', the bond of common vulnerability to change and experience uniting all creatures. 'To a Mouse' expresses sympathetic concern for its subject, and also awareness that despite man's power when compared with the rest of creation, he too is subject to fear and insecurity.

COMMENTARY:
The personal tone established by the first line of the poem, in which Burns speaks to a mouse, succeeds in communicating immediately the poet's sensitive recognition that the mouse is in a state of acute distress. This tender approach is maintained throughout. To a casual observer the incident of a very small animal having been turned up by the plough might seem unimportant; but Burns quickly understands that the mouse is both terrified and homeless. Identifying with the little accident victim quivering before him, he sincerely apologises in stanza 2 for the fact that mankind has failed to remember how much people and animals have in common. What follows is a series of heartfelt reflections on the vulnerability which mice and men share, despite the latter's appearance of being safe and strong. The mouse feels time present as catastrophic, but is at least spared anxiety about the future, unlike the poet himself.

NOTES AND GLOSSARY:
sleeket:	sleek
cowran:	cowering
tim'rous:	fearful

beastie:	little creature
breastie:	little breast
brattle:	sound of scamper
wad be laith to rin:	would be loath to run
pattle:	plough-staff
daimen-icker:	occasional ear
thrave:	24 sheaves
sma':	small
wi' the lave:	with what's left
silly wa's the win's:	frail walls the winds
big:	build
foggage:	rank grass
Baith snell:	both intensely cold
wast:	waste
coulter:	iron cutter of plough
stibble:	stubble
But . . . hald:	without refuge
thole:	endure
cranreuch:	hoar-frost
no thy-lane:	not alone
Gang aft agley:	often go wrong
e'e:	eye

'Epistle to Davie'

A poem written in the depths of winter which begins by recording Burns's bitter awareness of what it is to lack the resources of '*Great-folk*', but then becomes much more cheerful as the poet remembers Nature's beauty, which is free to everybody, and especially friendship, and love, both of which he enjoys. He declares that social rank, wealth, and learning do not confer lasting happiness. Emotion is paramount. The heart is always the part of humanity which makes people right or wrong. This leads him to urge Davie to join him in accepting their lot in life, encouraged by the pleasures of the heart.

COMMENTARY:

This poem is a good example of Burns's use of home-spun philosophy, to encourage himself as much as the friend he is addressing. Stanza 1 ends by stating honestly that Burns cannot prevent himself from envying the easy wealth and privileges of the great. Empty social pride angers him; he feels sour at seeing how unfairly things are shared. Even so, he and Davie are fit to work, and personally honest. They have the freedom to admire hills, woods, valleys, and 'foaming floods', and further to try out tunes and rhymes for their own pleasure. Stanza 5 presents the belief which gives unity to the entire poem: happiness comes not through having money, social position, or learning, but from the heart. The well-to-do are guilty of neglecting their fellow creatures; but Burns and Davie can learn to acquiesce cheerfully in their fate, and even to learn from misfortunes. Each has a loving female partner, and he and Davie are true friends to each other. For these reasons the poet ends by feeling freshly inspired. The imagery is homely and direct whenever possible, and the language and structure free from unnecessary complexity. Burns uses a 14-line stanza, in the manner of 'The Cherrie and the Slae', a sixteenth-century Scots poem.

NOTES AND GLOSSARY:

frae:	from
blaw:	blow
snaw:	snow
hing:	make us hang
ingle:	fireside
westlin:	westland
blaw in the drift:	blow in the fallen snow
Ben:	in
chimla lug:	chimney corner
bien:	comfortable
snug:	comfortable
tent:	heed
hanker, and canker:	become peevish
body's:	person's
chiels:	fellows
Coofs:	fools
rant:	roister
ken:	know
wair't:	spend
fash:	trouble
gear:	money
hale and fier:	healthy and sound
Mair:	more
spier:	ask
feg:	fig
warst:	worst
banes:	bones
ba':	ball
ay:	always
mind:	remember
But:	without
hal':	refuge
braes:	hillsides

sowth:	try over with a low whistle
Syne:	then
till't:	to it
Lear:	learning
lang:	for long
Wha:	who
An's:	and am
cartes:	cards
beets:	kindles
tenebrific:	dark and gloomy
skelpan:	spanking
rins:	runs
As:	as if
glowran:	gazing
spavet:	spavined, halting
het:	hot
hilch:	hobble
stilt:	limp
jimp:	jump
unco fit:	uncommon pace
least:	lest
dight:	wipe
wizen'd:	shrunk

'To a Mountain-Daisy'

A poem expressing concern for a daisy, crushed by the plough, which bears a general resemblance to the earlier 'To a Mouse'. The plough is involved in both texts; and just as he saw human parallels to the mouse, Burns compares the daisy, first to a vulnerable girl, and then to himself.

COMMENTARY:

'To a Mountain-Daisy' is clearly modelled on 'To a Mouse'. Noticeable at once is the similarity of language between the first line,

Wee, modest, crimson-tipped flow'r

and

Wee, sleeket, cowran, tim'rous beastie.

Significantly, the subtitles of the two poems in the 1786 Kilmarnock edition also show that the resemblance is more than accidental:

On turning her up in her Nest, with the Plough, November, 1785

and

On turning one down, with the Plough, in April – 1786.

The ideas which the poet seeks to express in 'To a Mountain-Daisy' mainly concern the similarity between the daisy and an over-trusting girl, who is betrayed by her lover, but the 'simple Bard' is also at the mercy of fate. There is little to suggest that this poem shares the originality of language, imagery and structure which gives distinction to 'To a Mouse'.

NOTES AND GLOSSARY:

stoure:	dust
weet:	wet
wa's:	wall's
maun:	must
bield:	shelter
stane:	stone
histie *stibble-field*:	bare stubble-field
alane:	alone
snawie:	snowy
share:	ploughshare

'Epistle to a Young Friend'

This is a poem which conveys lessons about living that are based on experience. Burns states that while most people are honest and trustworthy, selfish considerations seriously distort judgement. It is vitally important, therefore, that his young friend should keep some things to himself and not be over-credulous. He should avoid illicit love as it 'petrifies the feeling'. Ambition has its place, as long as it does not clash with what is honourable. Religion strengthens the promptings of conscience.

COMMENTARY:
Stanza 2 marks the real opening of the poem. Burns warns his friend that human beings are strange ('an unco squad'). He should expect care and trouble. Wicked people are few, but despite the good intentions of the majority, weakness is common. It is essential to be discreet, even with friends, while observing others keenly. Stanza 6 recommends love as wholesome, while advising strongly against illicit relationships. Court Fortune assiduously, the poet urges, as long as you use honest means, with the aim of becoming independent. Conscience, based on a sense of what belongs to honour, shows the clear difference between right and wrong. With regard to religion, the poet does not advise either fanatical belief or disrespect, but instead the anchor of 'A correspondence fix'd wi' Heav'n'. Burns makes use of a double stanza, balancing the sentiment of the first four lines in the second. He presents an image of himself as a keen-sighted observer of others.

NOTES AND GLOSSARY:

unco squad:	a strange group
muckle:	much
Poortith:	poverty
neebor's:	neighbour's
aff han':	offhand
keek:	look, pry
lowe:	flame
tempt:	attempt
waive the quantum:	ignore the amount
gear:	money, property
haud:	hold
ranting:	frolicking
reck the *rede*:	heed the advice

'To a Louse'

The purpose of this poem is social satire. Noticing in church that a louse has climbed onto the bonnet of Jenny, a girl who clearly takes pride in her fashionable appearance, Burns pretends to scold the insect, then comments sharply on the ways in which as human beings we deceive ourselves by not being able to see ourselves as others see us.

COMMENTARY:

Burns conveys vividly the impression created on him in church by a louse's presence close to Jenny. Her gauze and lace are mentioned in the first stanza, and she is referred to in the next stanza as a fine *lady*. The louse is scolded for daring to climb not into a beggar's hair, which could be expected, the poet claims, but on top of a young lady's bonnet, in the style of Lunardi's balloon – the very height of fashion. It is only in the final twelve lines that Burns lets his readers learn the true subject of the poem, which turns on human weakness. An unexpected minor incident is made a means of showing how people can deceive themselves through excessive vanity.

NOTES AND GLOSSARY:

crowlan ferlie:	crawling wonder
sairly:	indeed
strunt:	strut
wonner:	wonder
saunt:	saint
daur:	dare
fit:	foot
Swith:	off!

haffet squattle:	temple squat
sprattle:	scramble
ither:	other
cattle:	beasts
shoals and nations:	families and tribes
bane **ne'er daur:**	bone never dare
haud:	keep
fatt'rels:	falderals
vera tapmost:	very topmost
bauld:	bold
grozet:	gooseberry
rozet:	resin
fell:	deadly
smeddum:	powder
dress your droddum:	thrash your backside
flainen toy:	flannel cap
aiblins:	perhaps
duddie:	ragged
wylecoat:	flannel veṡt
Lunardi:	balloon bonnet
dinna:	do not
a' abread:	all abroad
blastie:	ill-disposed creature
Thae:	those
giftie:	little gift
lea'e:	leave

'Epistle to John Lapraik'

This poem shows Burns taking the initiative in writing to a stranger, of whom he has heard good reports, to seek his friendship. It contains a spirited account of the poet's literary beliefs and personal values.

COMMENTARY:
The occasion on which Burns first heard Lapraik's name is mentioned at the beginning. Burns was instinctively interested in someone who, like himself, had written poetry, and decided there and then that he must communicate with Lapraik. We learn that he began writing verse in childhood, and that he is committed to writing, whatever the assumptions made by 'Critic-folk' with more formal learning. A single spark of natural fire is all he needs in order to touch the heart; he prays for the inspiration of Ramsay or Fergusson, his immediate Scottish predecessors in poetry. He is aware of having one personal fault, a weakness for the girls. Declaring his positive wish to meet and exchange rhyming-ware with

Lapraik, say at Mauchline Race or Mauchline Fair, he adds that mutual support and friendship is his code, not coining money. He writes to Lapraik in the broad Scots understood by both, and brings in examples of the imagery of rural life.

NOTES AND GLOSSARY:

Paitricks scraichan:	partridges screaming
Poossie whiddan:	hare scudding
Fasteneen:	Shrove Tuesday
rockin:	spinning party
ca' the crack:	have a chat
yokin:	set-to
sang about:	singing in turns
Aboon:	above
thirl'd:	thrilled
wark:	work
tale:	told
chiel:	fellow
pat me fidgean-fain:	made me tingle with excitement
spier't:	asked
kent:	knew
ingine:	wit, ingenuity
douse:	sober
swoor an aith:	swore an oath
pleugh an' graith:	plough and harness
cadger pownie's:	hawker pony's
dyke-back:	behind a stone wall
baith:	both
crack:	talk
crambo-jingle:	rhyming
a body's sel:	oneself
sairs:	serves
shools:	shovels
knappin-hammers:	stone-breaking hammers
Hashes:	dunderheads
Stirks:	young bullocks
syne:	then
dub:	mud
spunk:	spark
bauld an' slee:	bold and clever
lear:	learning
fow:	full
I'se:	I'll
gif:	if

winna blaw:	will not brag
fauts:	faults
roose:	praise
Gude forgie:	God forgive
Plack:	coin
We'se:	we'll
chap:	cup
gar:	make
kirs'n:	christen
reekin:	steaming
whitter:	draught
warly:	worldly
havins:	manners
catch-the-plack:	coining money
dinna:	do not
gar me fissle:	make me tingle

'To the Same'

Three weeks after his first poem to Lapraik, Burns writes again. He is tired by the physically demanding labour of farming, which makes it tempting not to begin to write poetry, but Lapraik's praise for his poetry is an incentive which he cannot ignore. For his new friend he will improvise, then, to the best of his ability. Rejecting the worldliness of men dedicated to mere money-making and social position, he states that honesty and sociability are his primary values, commends poets, despite their poverty, and concludes by wishing well to Lapraik and himself.

COMMENTARY:
The first point of interest of this poem lies in its brief but candidly sketched opening, in which Burns reveals that farming makes it difficult for him to find the time and energy to write. He personifies his Muse in stanza 2, and presents in the next three stanzas his tired disinclination to write in the form of a telling-off spoken to his Muse. Scribbling down the idle talk that comes to mind is all he promises Lapraik, but what follows includes clear autobiographical evidence of the strength of his determination to keep his own values and to resist the self-seeking materialism of city-gents and haughty lords. Characteristic also is the language of the poem, rich in country humour.

NOTES AND GLOSSARY:

new-ca'd kye:	newly calved cattle
rowte:	low
pownies reek:	ponies smoke

braik:	harrow
Forjesket sair:	sorely jaded with fatigue
naigs:	nags
tapetless, ramfeezl'd hizzie: heedless, exhausted hussy	
dowf:	weak
pat:	put
thowless jad:	spiritless wench
blaud:	long, dull piece of writing
bauld:	bold
Roose:	praise
stumpie:	worn quill pen
clink:	rhyme
blether:	idle talk
aff-loof:	unpremeditated
kittle:	tickle
waft an' *warp*:	weave
jirt an' fleg:	jerk and scare
striddle:	straddle
lyart pow:	grey head
dow:	can
simmer:	summer
timmer:	wood
limmer:	jade
kittle kimmer:	fickle woman
kist:	counter
sklent:	squint
muckle wame:	big belly
bit *Brugh*:	small town
Baillie:	magistrate
paughty:	proud
sark:	shirt
-shank bane:	-leg bone
cits:	townsmen
remead:	remedy
gate:	way
nievefu':	fistful

'To W. S****n'

Burns has been embarrassed by an educated stranger's commendation of his poems. He cannot accept direct comparison with such distinguished earlier eighteenth-century Scottish poets as Ramsay and Gilbertfield, nor with his own near contemporary Fergusson, whose unhappy fate in Edinburgh he records. On the other hand, he wants the part of Ayrshire in which he has grown up to be well known for its poetry, and shows by example how strongly he responds to the beauty of Nature.

COMMENTARY:

A poem written in answer to a letter of praise from William Simson, who taught at Ochiltree in Ayrshire after a period of study at Glasgow University. Burns for his part praises the poetry of Allan Ramsay, Hamilton of Gilbertfield, and Robert Fergusson, whose recent early death he deplores. He invites Simson to join him in creating for Ayrshire's rivers Irwin, Lugar, Aire, and Doon poetic fame to be compared with that of the Yarrow and Tweed in Scotland, and with the poetic reputation elsewhere of the Ilissus, Tiber, Thames, and Seine. With this in view, the inspiring features of Coila or Kyle, his own central part of Ayrshire, are enthusiastically described. In a postscript, he gives Simson a mock-historic account of differences in belief within the Church of Scotland which explain the meaning of the terms 'old' and 'new licht'. The poem conveys pride in the part of Scotland which Burns knows best, and strong poetic ambition.

NOTES AND GLOSSARY:

brawlie:	heartily
billie:	fellow
I'se:	I'll
sud:	should
laith:	loath
sidelins sklented:	sideways directed
Musie:	Muse
sic phraisin:	extravagant
creel:	whirl
speel:	climb
braes:	slopes
writer-chiel:	lawyer chap
whunstane:	whinstone
Enburgh:	Edinburgh
tythe:	tenth
stow'd:	stored
screed:	rent
dead:	death
kittle:	tickle or touse
COILA:	the Muse of Kyle
fidge fu' fain:	tingle with delight
Bardies:	poets
ain:	own
Chiels:	fellows
winna hain:	will not spare

New Holland:	Australia
Besouth:	south of
aboon:	up
fit:	foot
cock:	hold up
gar:	make
burnies:	streamlets
Aft bure the gree:	bore off the prize
Suthron billies:	Englishmen
red-wat-shod:	shod with wet blood
haughs:	hollows
lintwhites:	linnets
jinkin:	sporting
whids:	gambols
cushat croods:	wood-pigeon coos
fand:	found
warly:	worldly
Hog-shouther:	push
jundie:	use elbows
descrive:	describe
Bum:	boast
brither:	brother
wallop in a tether:	be hanged in a noose
braxies:	dead sheep
preen:	pin
herds:	shepherds
callans:	striplings
braid lallans:	vernacular Lowland Scots
thae:	these
sark:	shirt
shoon:	shoes
Woor by degrees:	wore out
roon:	round
chiels:	fellows
wrang:	wrong
beuk:	book
threap:	insist
misteuk:	mistook
newk:	corner
backlins:	backwards
leuk:	look
hissels:	flocks
laddies:	boys
aiths:	oaths

clours:	bumps
licks:	punishment
crunt:	blow
learn:	teach
brunt:	burned
caddies:	rascals
bure:	bore
took the sands:	fled
cowe:	trouncing
stick-an-stowe:	utterly
knowe:	hillock
greetan:	weeping
girnan:	complaining
cowe the louns:	scare the rogues
neebor:	neighbouring
le'ae:	leave
shaird:	shard
pouch:	pocket
tulzie:	squabble
brulzie:	brawl

'It was upon a Lammas night'

This song is characteristic of Burns in two ways, in that it expresses love directly, and makes use of a seventeenth-century tune very much in keeping with the words which it helped to inspire.

COMMENTARY:
Burns stated that this song was written before his twenty-third year. He achieves a note of delight in remembered passion, especially in stanzas 2, 3, and 4, while the chorus matches the jaunty spirit of the entire lyric. Who Annie was is not known for certain, but the youngest daughter of John Rankine, a farmer in Burns's neighbourhood, subsequently claimed that she was the subject of the song. The chorus is a key feature of this song, as of others, and the verse of the entire song is handled with poise.

NOTES AND GLOSSARY:

Lammas:	harvest
rigs:	rows
bonie:	attractive
awa:	away
tentless:	careless
Amang:	among
ken't:	knew

ain:	own
owre:	over
ay:	always
hae:	have
gear:	cash, property

'Now westlin winds, and slaught'ring guns'

An unusual song for Burns in his twenties in that it is written in English, rather than in Scots or in a combination of the two. Later, Burns revised the song to include Scots diction. It is also untypical of love-songs in general in containing in stanza 3 four lines of direct protest against the shooting of birds.

COMMENTARY:
Written in 1775 when Burns visited the village of Kirkoswald in southern Ayrshire and fell in love with a girl called Peggy Thomson. Love which Burns claims is enjoyed by different kinds of creature gives thematic unity to the lyric, and no doubt he writes in large part to persuade Peggy that it is natural for a young couple like themselves to follow instinct. What makes the song different from many other love-songs is the writer's strong and explicit condemnation of the killing of wildfowl which Burns knew to be practised in the name of sport.

NOTES AND GLOSSARY:
westlin: westerly
Cushat: wood-pigeon

'A Bard's Epitaph'

A poem of wry self-awareness, in which Burns acknowledges errors of judgement which prevent him from living up to his own ideal of self-control. Perhaps because the poem is described as an epitaph, he chooses to write all but two lines of the first stanza in English.

COMMENTARY:
The poem projects an image of someone possessing intelligence and creative ability, but also an impulsive nature that could lead him into making foolish mistakes. These, the writer believes, have repeatedly prevented him from fulfilling his potential. Burns presents himself in terms of inner contradictions, and is candid about the 'thoughtless follies' which have coloured his relationships with girls. He is concerned to pass on to others teaching which he feels he has failed to practise himself. The language of the short poem is mainly English.

NOTES AND GLOSSARY:

owre:	too
blate:	diffident
snool:	submit
dool:	lament
drap:	drop
this area:	i.e. the churchyard
frater-:	brother-

'Holy Willie's Prayer'

This satire is directed both against a particular individual known to Burns, and against the hypocritical attitudes he represents. So famous did the poem become that 'a Holy Willie' has entered the language.

COMMENTARY:
Burns begins by quoting a line from Pope, English master of poetic satire in the first half of the eighteenth century. In form, 'Holy Willie's Prayer' is a dramatic monologue, conveying the poet's own very different critical viewpoint by means of the speech and thoughts of an invented character. Willie Fisher is made to utter statements, in the name of religion, which by turn are self-righteous, lustful, and aggressive – scarcely amounting to a pattern or model of Christian love or restraint. Burns attacks Fisher by using the traditional sequence in prayers of invocation and praise (lines 1–30); confession and penitence (lines 37–60); intercession and petition (lines 61–102). The misapplication by Willie of what was made familiar to Burns's contemporaries through worship in church is steeped in irony. Thus Willie's petition contains both a series of requests for harsh vengeance against his enemies, and an essentially materialistic request that he himself may shine 'for grace and gear' (line 100). The language and structure of the poem completely undermine the individual and attitude Burns satirises.

NOTES AND GLOSSARY:

gooms:	gums
fash'd:	afflicted
maun:	must
fou:	drunk
cartes:	cards
splore:	uproar
kail:	cabbage
hingin:	hanging

'Tam o' Shanter'

This was Burns's own favourite among his poems, and within a few years of its first publication in 1791 it became a great success with readers and listeners alike. Its popularity has never diminished, as reflected by the fact that the poem is still recited around the world every year on Burns Night. Tam o' Shanter, a farmer, spends the evening after Ayr market in a pleasant inn with his crony Souter Johnny, flirting with the innkeeper's wife and oblivious of his own wife Kate's warnings about his weakness for drink and idle talk. At midnight the weather is stormy when Tam has to set out to ride home on his trusty mare Meg. He is puzzled by mysterious lights at Kirk-Alloway. It turns out that warlocks and witches are dancing to the bagpipes, played by Old Nick, the Devil. Tam finds himself strongly attracted by the scantily clad Nannie, the only young witch in the company. When however he shouts to congratulate her on her dancing, the lights go out and the witches set out after Tam, who is terrified. Spurring on Meg wildly, he reaches the safety of the old bridge over the Doon, but the mare's tail is still in the area controlled by the furious young witch, who leaves poor Meg 'scarce a stump'.

COMMENTARY:
Line 5 gives an early indication that Burns identifies with Tam, the central figure of the poem: an English translation is 'we sit boozing'. Sympathy between the poem's hero and its creator is implied from the start. 'Tam o' Shanter' accepts human failings, especially drink and sex. Tam experiences an extraordinary adventure, but he represents ordinary, credulous humanity. He has earned his wife's disapproval by spending long hours drinking with his crony Souter Johnny and flirting with women, including, on the very day of the story, the unnamed wife of an Ayr innkeeper. As the tale develops, the supernatural comes to the fore as a principal part of the narrative, but above all this is to be read as a poem of laughter and acceptance. Sex and drink are central to its meaning. That said, there is considerable art in the way Burns varies the narrative voices used in 'Tam o' Shanter'. Though simple in the best sense, it is a complex piece of work, one which is deliberately created for spoken performance, yet subtly poetic in its imagery. An example of Burns's adroit control of idiom occurs in the way he describes Nannie's appearance and dancing, lines 171–84. (See also detailed commentary on this poem on pp. 74–6.)

NOTES AND GLOSSARY:
chapman billies:　pedlar lads
drouthy neebors:　thirsty neighbours
tak the gate:　take the road
bousing at the nappy: boozing ale

fou:	drunk
unco:	very
slaps:	gaps in walls
fand:	found
Auld:	old
ain:	own
tauld:	told
weel:	well
skellum:	rascal
blellum:	babbler
ilka melder:	every time for corn-grinding
siller:	silver
naig was ca'd a shoe:	nag was shod
catch'd:	caught
mirk:	darkness
gars me greet:	makes me weep
unco:	just
ingle, bleezing:	fireside, blazing
reaming swats:	foaming beer
Souter:	shoemaker
lo'ed:	loved
vera brither:	very brother
thegither:	together
drave:	drove
clatter:	gossip
tauld:	told
rair:	roar
E'en:	even
flee:	fly
lades:	loads
-stane:	-stone
'twad blawn:	if blowing
Deil:	Devil
skelpit:	hurried
dub:	mud
bogles:	ghosts
gaists and houlets:	ghosts and owls
snaw:	snow
smoor'd:	smothered
birks and meikle stane:	birches and large stone
brak's neck-bane:	broke his neckbone
whins:	gorse
bairn:	child
aboon:	above

mither:	mother
bore:	crevice
tippeny:	ale at two old pence a pint
usquabae:	whisky
ream'd:	foamed
noddle:	head
boddle:	worthless coin
sair:	sorely
brent:	brand
strathspeys:	Scottish dance
winnock-bunker:	window-seat
auld Nick:	The Devil
towzie tyke:	ragged mongrel
gie:	give
gart them skirl:	made them shriek
dirl:	shake
presses:	cupboards
shaw'd:	showed
cantraip:	magic, trick
cauld:	cold
haly:	holy
banes in gibbet-airns:	bones in gibbet-irons
span-lang:	nine-inch i.e. small
rape:	rope
gab:	mouth
blude:	blood
stack:	stuck
cleekit:	linked arms
ilka carlin:	each old witch
swat and reekit:	sweated and reeked
coost her duddies to the wark:	cast her rags to the work
sark:	slip, shift
queans:	young girls
creeshie flannen:	greasy flannel
snaw-white:	best
Thir breeks:	these trousers
ance:	once
hurdies:	buttocks
ae blink:	one glimpse
burdies:	girls
beldams:	hags
Rigwoodie:	withered
spean:	wean
Lowping:	leaping

crummock:	crook
fu' brawlie:	full well
wawlie:	good-looking
kend:	knew
baith:	both
bear:	barley
cutty sark:	short slip
harn:	linen
vauntie:	proud
coft:	bought
twa pund:	two pounds
Wad:	would have
cour:	cower
lap and flang:	leapt and kicked
souple jade:	supple wench
een:	eyes
fidg'd fu' fain:	twitched with excitement
hotched:	fidgeted
ae:	one
syne:	then
tint:	lost
bizz:	buzz
fyke:	commotion
byke:	hive
eldritch skreech:	unearthly shriek
fairin:	just reward
brig:	bridge
fient a:	never a
ettle:	aim
hale:	completely
o'er:	too

'Death and Dr Hornbook'

The poet is on his way home after a convivial evening when he has an unexpected meeting in the moonlight with Something. The mysterious figure turns out to be none other than Death, which at first terrifies the poet, who while not drunk – by his own reckoning, at any rate – is not completely sober, either. Death tells him of a serious professional grievance he has had to endure from a rival, Dr Hornbook. Hornbook who has set himself up as the local apothecary, is killing more people than Death. The latter is vowing solemnly that he will get the better of Hornbook when the clock ends the poet's talk with Death by striking one in the morning.

COMMENTARY:
This poem is in part a personal satire at the expense of John Wilson, a local apothecary who both irritated and amused Burns in 1785 by making exaggerated claims about his medical skills, but more significantly a comic tale which reduces fear of the supernatural. In that sense it resembles the more famous 'Tam o' Shanter'; and it is a significant part of the opening situation of the narrative that the narrator has been drinking, just as Tam has been drinking in Burns's other verse tale. Essentially, 'Death and Dr Hornbook' robs Death of the power to instil fear among superstitious country people by creating an absurd situation of rivalry between him and Dr Hornbook. Death is portrayed as laughably prone to petty jealousy. He has no more dignity than the narrator of the poem, who is clearly tipsy – see the third stanza.

NOTES AND GLOSSARY:

kenn'd:	known
vend:	sell
gaun:	going
Clachan yill:	village ale
canty:	contented
fou:	drunk
stacher'd whyles:	staggered at times
tent ay:	care always
Frae ghaists:	from ghosts
-owre:	over
cou'd na:	could not
todlin:	tottering
sicker:	sure
bicker:	rush
pat:	put
eerie swither:	frightened doubt
-owre ae shouther:	over one shoulder
-tae'd:	-toed
leister:	dart for catching fish
ither:	other
lang:	long
ells:	measures of length
fient:	no
wame:	stomach
ava:	at all
branks:	rustic horse bridles
Guid-een:	good evening
mawin:	mowing
sawin:	sowing

naething spak:	said nothing
howe:	hollow
fley'd:	afraid
stap:	stop
tent:	attend to
billie:	my man
red:	advise
weel:	well
skaith:	injury
gully:	large knife
whittle:	knife
wad:	would
kittle:	likely
mislear'd:	misunderstood
gies:	give
sae:	so
gree't:	agree
hae:	have
mony:	many
lang:	long
maun:	must
Sax:	six
stap:	stop
Hornbook:	sheet for teaching the alphabet
waur:	worst
Clachan:	village
king's-hood:	part of ox entrails
spleuchan:	tobacco pouch
sae weel:	so well
Buchan:	*Buchan's Domestic Medicine*
weans haud:	children hold
pouk:	pluck
D--n'd haet:	nothing
yestreen:	last night
gaen:	gone
deil-ma-care:	for all that
dirl:	knock
bane:	bone
Fient haet:	nothing
kail-runt:	cabbage-stem
cowpit:	tumbled
bauld:	bold
whin-rock:	hard rock
kail-blade:	cabbage leaf

Calces:	powders
whittles:	knives
hae:	have
Sal-marinum:	sea-salt
Farina of beans:	vegetable meal
aqua-fontis:	fresh water
Forbye:	as well as
Urinus Spiritus:	urine
sal-alkali:	salt
Waes me for:	alas!
braw:	fine-looking
calf-ward:	small enclosure for calves
rive:	dig up
grain'd:	groaned
eldritch:	weird
pleugh:	plough
eneugh:	enough
a':	all
trench'd:	dug
sheugh:	ditch
strae-death:	death in bed
claith:	cloth, shroud
Wabster:	weaver
nieves:	fists
tippence-:	twopence-
sair:	sore
slade:	did slide
cannie:	mild
batts:	colic
curmurring:	murmuring
twa:	two
guid:	good
gimmer-pets:	young ewes kept as pets
hov'd:	swelled
aff:	off
lang hame:	death
swatch:	sample
An 's weel:	and is well
Niest:	next
groat:	small coin
wad:	bit
fairin:	just reward
strak:	struck
ayont the *twal*:	beyond twelve

Songs

'Ae fond kiss'

This is one of Burns's most famous songs, inspired (along with nine other songs) by his love for 'Clarinda', Mrs Nancy McLehose, a noted beauty of whom Burns saw much in Edinburgh in 1787–8, and who had left her husband because of his cruelty. The poet sent her this song shortly after their last meeting in Edinburgh in December 1791. Mrs McLehose was to write in her Journal forty years later, on 6 December 1831: 'This day I can never forget. Parted with Burns, in the year 1791, never more to meet in this world. Oh, may we meet in Heaven!' The tune, Rory Dall's Port, was known to Burns from the *Caledonian Pocket Companion*, 1756, viii. 24. Rory Dall was the name given to the harpers attached to the Macleods of Skye. 'Port' is Gaelic for 'air'.

COMMENTARY:
What makes the words of this song stand out in popular tradition and be very widely remembered, in contrast to those of dozens of other love-songs? In part, it can certainly be argued that this lyric has biographical appeal. Among Burns's many love affairs, his unconsummated relation-ship with Nancy McLehose has a poignancy of its own. More important, though, the words of 'Ae fond kiss' impress listeners and readers alike as heartfelt, expressing true emotion. Stanza 4 especially has been judged to convey shared ardent feeling succinctly and movingly. Sir Walter Scott comments on lines 13–16:

> Had we never lov'd sae kindly,
> Had we never lov'd sae blindly!
> Never met – or never parted,
> We had ne'er been broken-hearted

that 'they contain the essence of a thousand love tales'. The song's final effect is of lasting passion, as its language shows to listeners and readers alike.

NOTES AND GLOSSARY:

Ae:	one
nae:	no
sae:	so
ilka:	every

'Mary Morison' (from *The Songs of Robert Burns*)

One of approximately thirty songs which predate the Kilmarnock edition. Hugh MacDiarmid (pen-name of the poet Christopher Grieve), who may be regarded as a gifted modern successor and rival to Burns in Scottish poetry, commented on 'the supreme power of Burns's finest line',

Ye are na Mary Morison.

He perhaps had in mind Burns's 'voice', the mastery of idiom in his use of colloquial speech to express deep feeling succinctly. Certainly the song clearly conveys Burns's longing to be in Mary's presence as her accepted lover.

COMMENTARY:
What distinguishes the song in its entirety is Burns's apt combination of images of sight and sound ('Yestreen when to the trembling string/The dance gaed through the lighted ha') with direct personal statement and a mood of wistful tenderness. Who Mary Morrison was has not been discovered by the poet's biographers. In one sense, her real-life identity scarcely matters. 'O Mary, at thy window be' works well as a lyric conveying the poet's admiration for Mary, and his passionate desire to exert himself on her behalf. Burns's song, however, is also a fine early attempt to marry words to music. Opening on a low note, it changes as it develops. In the fifth line, the address to Mary is intensified, and Burns's words express the character of the tune. The language of the song aptly conveys the writer's high regard for the girl he praises.

NOTES AND GLOSSARY:

trysted:	chosen for meeting
wad:	would
bide:	put up with
stoure:	dust
frae:	from
Yestreen:	yesterday evening
gaed:	went
ha':	hall
braw:	attractive
yon:	that one
Ye are na:	you are not
Wha:	who
faute:	fault
gie:	give

'The rantin dog the Daddie o't' (from *The Songs of Robert Burns*)

A song expressing what its writer, a man, hoped might be the attitude of the young woman who is supposed to be the speaker. Despite having certain practical worries, she is ready to share with him the church's public disapproval of their sexual relationship, and eagerly anticipates a renewal of love-making after bearing his child.

COMMENTARY:
The language of the song conveys awareness that the birth of a child outside marriage was seen as a disgrace by the Church. Burns commented, 'I composed this song pretty early in life, and sent it to a young girl, a very particular acquaintance of mine, who was at that time under a cloud' (*Notes on Scottish Song*, p. 50). 'O, wha my babie-clouts will buy?' could have been written either for Elizabeth Paton or for Jean Armour. The song was partly modelled on 'The Cordial', a wooing dialogue by Allan Ramsay which includes the question, 'Will ye tent [heed] me when I cry?', but Burns's handling of the theme, in which the girl expresses defiant loyalty to her lover and looks forward to further love-making, is strongly original.

NOTES AND GLOSSARY:

-clouts:	-clothes
rantin:	riotous
groanin maut:	ale at a birth
ca 't:	call it
Creepie-chair:	stool of repentance
crack:	chat
my lane:	on my own
fidgin fain:	eager

'There was a lad' (from *The Songs of Robert Burns*)

A version of this song, with minor variations from the one collected by Cromek, exists in Burns's Second (Edinburgh) Commonplace Book. The song was probably written in late January 1787 in wry celebration of the poet's birthday, which he mentions in a footnote to line 11. Burns had obviously been told by his parents of the great storm in Alloway in January 1759. For the rest, he relies on his sense of humour and ironic self-awareness. Gilbert Burns wrote of the damage done to their home.

When my father built his 'clay biggin', he put in two stone-jambs, as they are called, and a lintel, carrying up the chimney in his clay-gable. The consequence was, that as the gable subsided, the jambs, remaining firm, threw it off centre; and, one very stormy morning, when my brother was nine or ten days old, a little before daylight, a part of the gable fell out, and the rest appeared so shattered, that my mother, with the young poet, had to be carried through the storm to a neighbour's house, where they remained a week, till their own dwelling was adjusted. (Quoted by F. B. Snyder, *The Life of Robert Burns*, 1932, p. 39.)

COMMENTARY:
Burns stated clearly that 'There was a lad was born in Kyle' was intended
to be set to the traditional tune *Dainty Davie*; but the song is usually sung,
following nineteenth-century practice, to a different air, *O an ye were dead
Gudeman*. The poet's explicit imagery and language convey his meaning
cheerfully.

NOTES AND GLOSSARY:

Kyle:	the central district of Ayrshire
what na:	what
Rantin':	riotous
hindmost:	last
Janwar' Win':	January wind
hansel:	New-Year or good-luck gift
Gossip:	neighbour-woman
keekit:	looked
loof:	palm
Quo' scho:	said she
waly:	handsome
coof:	fool
mak:	make
ilka:	each
our kin':	our sex
leeze me on:	I am delighted by
stir:	sir
aspar:	with legs apart

'Afton Water' (from *The Songs of Robert Burns*)

Burns sent a copy of 'Flow gently, sweet Afton' to Mrs Dunlop on
5 February 1789, with this note on the river which inspired it:

> There is a small river, Afton, that falls into Nith, near New Cumnock;
> which has some charming, wild, romantic scenery on its banks – I have
> a particular pleasure in those little pieces of poetry such as our Scots
> songs &c. where the names and landskip-features of rivers, lakes, or
> woodlands, that one knows, are introduced. – I attempted a compliment
> of that kind, to Afton as follows: I mean it for Johnson's *Musical
> Museum* (letter 310, *Letters*, I 370).

COMMENTARY:
Burns loved running water. This song expresses intense affection both for
his loved one and for the river Afton.

There has been much debate as to the real-life identity of 'Mary'.
Burns's brother Gilbert believed that she was Mary Campbell, 'Highland
Mary'. At any rate, she is associated with the Afton and its banks.

The air would appear to have been first published in the *Scots Musical Museum*.

NOTES AND GLOSSARY:
braes: hillsides
birk: birch

'Tam Glen' (from *The Songs of Robert Burns*)

Burns wrote to Mrs Dunlop in December 1788,

> I shall give you a song I finished the other day, & sent it to Johnson for his Publication. – It sings to an excellent old lilt, known in Oswald's Collection of Scots Music by the name of, 'The merry beggars'. – I would give a bottle of wine to hear it sung . . .'

Robert Riddell described the song as 'this droll and expressive description of the feelings of a love-sick country girl' (*Notes on Scottish Song*, p. 70).

COMMENTARY:
The appeal of the song lies in the girl's single-minded preoccupation with Tam Glen. She sees him as her destined lover whatever her parents may think. Theology ('if it's ordain'd I maun tak him') and superstition ('the last Halloween . . .') both point in the same direction. A nice touch is the reference to Lowrie the laird o' Dumeller. Like the awkward suitor Dumbiedykes in Scott's *The Heart of Midlothian*, he is a man with more silver to offer than gracious words. Burns's attitude in the song is light-hearted and playful.

NOTES AND GLOSSARY:
Tittie: sister
len': lend
poortith: poverty
mak a fen': make do
mauna: must not
laird: squire
ben: indoors
blaws: boasts
siller: silver
Minnie: mother
deave: deafen
gin: if
hunder: hundred
Yestreen: yesterday evening
mou: mouth
gied: gave

sten:	leap
Halloween:	eve of All Saints' Day
waukin:	waking
droukit:	drenched
sark-:	shirt
staukin:	stalking
breeks:	trousers

'Ay waukin O' (from *The Songs of Robert Burns*)

This celebrated song describes in simple language the wakefulness caused not by the season, which happens to be summer, but by unhappy love.

COMMENTARY:
One of Burns's most poignant love songs. It is based on a traditional fragment

Sleep I can get nane
For thinking on my dearie.
A' the night I wak,
A' the day I weary,
Sleep I can get nane
For thinkin on my dearie.

Burns has expanded this idea, keeping the mood of the original (and in his chorus the phrasing), and perfectly matching the whole song to a slow air, which probably dates from before the eighteenth century. If a lyric succeeds when it expresses a single idea eloquently, it is because the words are chosen with distinction.

NOTES AND GLOSSARY:

Simmer:	summer
rins:	runs
heugh:	steep bank
waukin:	waking
Dearie:	beloved
irie:	apprehensive
Lanely:	lonely
lave:	the rest

'A red red Rose' (from *The Songs of Robert Burns*)

A world-famous love song which combines images drawn from the natural world – a rose and ocean – with the poet's exceptional understanding of melody.

COMMENTARY:
Burns begins by naming a rose, then adds a sweetly played melody, because he wants to convey his loved one's beauty. Her beauty is matched by his ardour, which is compared to the enduring vitality of the world's seas. He claims that while the sands of life shall run, so will his love, and he will come again, even if the distance were ten thousand miles. What stands out about his imagery is its simplicity, which carries conviction as elaborate diction would not.

NOTES AND GLOSSARY:

bonie:	attractive
a':	all
gang:	go
fare thee weel:	farewell

'Auld lang syne' (from *The Songs of Robert Burns*)

A world-famous song of parting, which conveys its meaning of loyal affection and friendship, despite the challenge of some unfamiliar Scots words and phrases. At least the chorus is earlier than Burns's day, belonging to a traditional song, but the poet gave verbal distinction to the completed song.

COMMENTARY:
A good eighteenth-century lyric flows from a single thought. In this instance, the poet asks a stunningly simple question: should old acquaintance be forgotten? The answer is no. The third and fourth verses give further clues to his skill in imparting depth and unity to the song. This friendship dates from childhood:

We twa hae run about the braes . . .
We twa hae paidl'd in the burn.

The imagery is universal. And thus he replies to the question decisively. Old acquaintance is not to be forgotten. Instead, it grows more precious and valuable with the passing of the years.

NOTES AND GLOSSARY:

auld:	old
lang syne:	long since, long ago
jo:	sweetheart
stowp:	tankard, measure
pou'd:	pulled
gowans:	daisy or dandelion flowers
fitt:	foot
paidl'd:	paddled

burn: stream
dine: dinner-time
braid: broad
fiere: companion
gude-willie-waught: cordial drink, cup of kindness

List of common words

a': all
ae: one
aft(en): often
amaist: almost
amang: among
ance: once
ane: one
auld: old
awa: away
ay(e): always
baith: both
ben: indoors/within
bluid: blood
bon(n)ie: attractive
braw: fine, splendid
ca': call
cauld: cold
countra: country
fa': fall
frae: from
gae, gaen, gaun: go, gone
gang: go
gat: got
gie: give
guid: good
hae: have
hame: home
ither: other
ilk(a): each, every
ken: know
lang(er): long(er)
mair: more
maist: most, almost
maun: must
meikle/mickle/muckle: much
monie: many

na, nae, nane, naething:	not, no, none, nothing
onie/ony:	any
owre:	over, too
sae:	so
sang:	song
sic/sich:	such
sma':	small
tae:	to
taen:	taken
thegither:	together
tither:	the other
twa:	two
unco:	very, odd
wa':	wall
wad:	would, would have
wee:	small
weel:	well
wha/whase:	who, whose
whare:	where
why(i)les:	now, at times, sometimes
yon:	that

Part 3

Commentary

Literary aims and themes

What were Burns's motives for writing poetry? Like many other poets before and since, he offered conflicting explanations at different points in his life. These reflect his changing moods, and particular contexts, in conversation, letters, and print. It is clear, however, that above all he rhymed for his own pleasure, just as – apparently without ever winning much praise for it – he enjoyed playing the fiddle. He began with a love-song, and from his teens had the habit of writing verses to impress girls and express 'the softer passions'. By his mid-twenties he was keenly interested in making his mark as one of the poets of his own district of Ayrshire. The matter might have rested there, save for the strong ambition natural in any young poet of outstanding ability. By the time he decided to bring out *Poems, Chiefly in the Scottish Dialect* at Kilmarnock in 1786, Burns had hopes that, even if he should not be lucky enough to attract much notice, he might be worthy of a place in Scottish poetry as a successor to Allan Ramsay and Robert Fergusson.

The Kilmarnock volume carries a Preface which makes it clear that the poet's first aim is to describe the way of life and values of country people like himself. He draws a distinction between his own intimate involvement with his subject and the very different approach of a learned poet amusing himself, 'perhaps amid the elegancies and idlenesses of upper life', by choosing 'a rural theme'. He has been led to celebrate the way of life and attitudes he has seen in himself and others sharing his background, 'in his and their native language'. Burns follows this characteristically truthful claim with an equally revealing explanation of his reasons for writing.

> To amuse himself with the little creations of his own fancy, amid the toils and fatigues of a laborious life; to transcribe the various feelings, the loves, the griefs, the hopes, the fears, in his own breast; to find some kind of counterpoise to the struggles of a world, always an alien scene, a task uncouth to the poetrical mind; these were his motives for courting the Muses, and in these he found Poetry to be its own reward.

Life was dauntingly hard for Burns and those fated like himself to wear the 'russet coat' of the working tenant farmer. In his case it was made all the more frustrating because he knew himself to have exceptional abilities, and yet was denied any real prospect of bettering himself. His letters and early poetry both show that he felt acutely the injustice of an economic and social system which offered scant opportunity to anyone born without capital. In itself, the writing of poetry might not succeed in bringing about a change either in his personal circumstances or in the distribution of wealth. It was, nevertheless, a congenial form of activity in its own right and one with much more purpose to it than mere dreaming. Through writing, Burns found a forward momentum and outlet for his ideas to set against the daily drudgery of working on the land.

Writing can be a form of therapy for the one who writes. In this same part of the Preface to his 1786 *Poems*, Burns explains that one of his reasons for writing poetry has been a need for self-expression, an instinct accepted as part of his nature 'to transcribe the various feelings, the loves, the griefs, the hopes, the fears in his own breast'. These words, with their emphasis on the authentic rendering of feeling, might almost be taken as the declaration of faith of any Romantic poet of the next generation. And indeed there is a sense in which even at the outset of his career, Burns was committed to self-affirmation in poetry to a degree which was very unusual at this date. A song such as 'It was upon a Lammas night', for example, is in no sense merely a 'literary' exercise, but instead a direct and intimate communication from the heart. Stanza 3 and the chorus especially make clear that the song has personal experience as the basis of its meaning:

> I lock'd her in my fond embrace;
>   Her heart was beating rarely:
> My blessings on that happy place,
>   Amang the rigs o' barley!
> But by the moon and stars so bright,
>   That shone that night so clearly!
> She ay shall bless that happy night,
>   Amang the rigs o' barley.

In this song Burns achieves with apparent ease what Keats was to describe as 'the true voice of feeling'. Remodelling a rather insipid and coy love-song of Allan Ramsay, and keeping in mind the fine folk-melody to which it is set the poet here is candidly and uninhibitedly autobiographical. Even without the tune – but much more fully when set to it – the lyric succeeds in capturing the ringing pride and delight of a real individual who has been lucky in love. Although its art conceals art, it lives up to Burns's claim in his Preface about his motives for writing by being a 'transcript' of joy, pure and simple.

Burns's voice as a poet is distinctively personal throughout his *Poems*. Time and again we hear what seem to be the accents of felt experience. His moods naturally vary. He may be at a high point of happiness, as in 'It was upon a Lammas night'. Or, quite differently, he may be fatigued at the end of the day and in need of fresh inspiration, as in the opening of 'The Vision. Duan First', where he muses on 'wast'd time', which he has spent 'stringing blethers up in rhyme', and the thought strikes him that he could instead have embarked on a financially rewarding career.

Had I to guid advice but harket,	listened
I might, by this, hae led a market,	by now
Or strutted in a Bank and clarket	written up
My *Cash-Account*	

The mood may change, but the poet's communicative frankness does not. Burns's wry humour in this passage is no less one of his characteristic ways of responding to experience than the carefree swagger of 'It was upon a Lammas night'. As it develops, 'The Vision. Duan First' faithfully enacts Burns's belief about poetry as a means of being creative in the face of adversity. The process described is one of widening one's personal horizons, which a committed poet may expect to be able to set against life's round of wearying tasks. Coila, who visits and encourages the poet, shows him that poetry is indeed 'its own reward'.

The most immediately noticeable feature of the description which opens 'The Vision. Duan First' is its sheer realism. The cottage and smoky fireside are there before our eyes. As well as having a remarkable gift for communicating feeling, Burns is skilled at creating a sense of the physical world about him. His curiosity extends in every direction, with human life at the centre of the scene. This balance of interests is characteristic. The first and most important strength of Burns's work is his clear-sighted observation – of himself, of others, and of the surrounding environment. He has followed the precept 'look in your heart and write', but without losing touch with external reality.

In his devotion to accurate recording of what he sees, as well as what he feels, Burns remains true to the values of the eighteenth century. His stress on emotion, especially in song, at times anticipates Romantic literary practice, but his outlook has been even more strongly influenced by the bracing combined effect of the realities of country living and of literary art as practised for example by Pope, whose poems he keenly admired. Much of his poetry belongs to mainstream eighteenth-century tradition.

Coila refers in 'The Vision. Duan First' to Burns's 'manners-painting strains'. Burns has in mind a truthful, positive rendering of the way of life and values by which members of a social group live. The emphasis on Scots is significant here; Burns has chosen to use the vernacular in certain poems both because he is at home in it and because he knows it to belong in an integral way to his subject. Examples of poems which describe 'manners' in this sense include 'The Twa Dogs. A Tale', 'The Holy Fair', and 'The Cotter's Saturday Night'. In each of these, while varying his poetic style and approach according to the topic, Burns follows the tradition of communal or *genre* painting on the one hand and of his Scots predecessor Robert Fergusson's poetry on the other by illustrating facets of the human comedy.

'The Twa Dogs. A Tale', which opens the book, admirably represents his art in that it expresses with considerable force and subtlety the poem's social meaning, by means of Scots dialogue and narrative. The poet's main purpose here is to communicate certain home truths about the yawning gulf in outlook and values between the life of rich and poor in rural Ayrshire. Burns deftly accomplishes this by making use of two dogs, who become his personae or characters in simulated debate.

'The Twa Dogs. A Tale' belongs to a long Scottish tradition of animal poems. Like his fifteenth-century predecessor Henryson in such fables as 'The Uponlandis Mous and the Burges Mous', about a country and a town mouse, Burns creates a special satirical effect by having animals talk. Caesar is a Newfoundland belonging to a rich estate-owner. Commendably free himself from any snobbish or exclusive spirit ('the fient a pride na pride had he'), he discloses to his companion the shortcomings of the wealthy – including snobbish pride – all of which he has seen at first hand.

In conversation with him is Luath, a poor ploughman's collie, named after an actual dog of the poet's. His role in the poem is to register shock at what he learns from Caesar, and to draw attention by contrast to positive qualities in the lives of the long-suffering poor, as in the remark that the latter are not as wretched as one might think. Though constantly on the brink of poverty, they make the most of scant leisure hours, and take pride in looking after their children. Moreover, they find intellectual stimulus in discussing church and state affairs, and wholeheartedly enjoy such social highlights as 'Kirns' (harvest-homes) and 'That *merry day* the year begins'. Overall, the poem establishes a dramatic contrast between worthy poor people determined to make the best of their circumstances, and the pampered rich, who have so much time on their hands that they do not know what to do with themselves.

'The Cotter's Saturday Night' differs from 'The Twa Dogs. A Tale' in that it is predominantly solemn in tone. 'Manners-painting' humour does occur, for instance in the treatment of the mother's pardonable pride in her cheese, but it is secondary and incidental. Another difference between the poems is related to this difference in tone. Whereas Scots is employed throughout 'The Twa Dogs. A Tale', Burns makes use of dignified English diction at certain points in 'The Cotter's Saturday Night'. This is not a sign of any false pretence or cultural betrayal on the poet's part, but is instead an accurate reflection of the linguistic habit of Scotland since the Scottish Reformation in the sixteenth century, when the English Bible was first adopted to be used in Scottish pulpits.

In its own way, 'The Cotter's Saturday Night' is remarkably true to what had for long been an accepted spoken norm in Scotland, namely the use of

Scots as the natural first choice for most secular purposes, and by contrast of English as the language of devotion and worship. Literary tradition had reinforced and accentuated the division before Burns's time. By alternating between his native Scots and passages of reflection in English, the poet simply develops in his own distinctive manner a stylistic variation already present in the literature he inherited from the past. Burns wishes to present the high point of the life of a family, namely their Saturday evening meal and worship. Scots and English diction are both an integral part of the appropriate poetic language he uses.

Robert Fergusson excels in rendering with satisfyingly exact and well-chosen Scots phrases a characteristic farmhouse kitchen interior in a poem entitled 'The Farmer's Ingle'. Burns builds on the example of Fergusson's poem, but adds an explicit emotional and religious dimension of his own. Specifically, he innovates by creating both Jenny's loving courtship and five stanzas about the family's act of worship, and invests much of the idealised picture with overtones of the 'domestic sublime'. The story of Jenny and her wooer introduces a narrative episode treating romantic love. This helped to broaden the poem's appeal in the Age of Sentiment when it was first published, and 'The Cotter's Saturday Night' remained very popular in the nineteenth century. On the other hand, more recent critics have criticised as hypocritical the repudiation of seduction in stanza 10 ('Is there, in human form, that bears a heart . . .') by a poet notorious for loose living. This raises the issue of the poet's sincerity or lack of it in a central part of the poem. 'The Cotter's Saturday Night' is fervently patriotic as well as moral, and this feature, especially in stanza 19, has also drawn adverse comment in the twentieth century.

It is surely evidence at least of a powerful current of life in the poem that its values and method continue to provoke debate. What is in danger of being missed in our own day in 'The Cotter's Saturday Night' is the depth of Burns's biblical knowledge and awareness of Scottish Presbyterian tradition. Stanza 13, for instance, provides a description of the family singing 'Scotia's holy lays'. Several of these are named; and historical research confirms that Burns has selected in *Dundee, Martyrs*, and *Elgin* three of the melodies which would indeed have been employed on such an occasion. There is a no less carefully worked out connection between the family values of the whole poem, clearly identifiable Old and New Testament texts which are cited by the poet, and the nature of the parents' prayer when they are alone.

Once again, and unexpectedly, Burns's thorough knowledge of the Bible is put to good use in the most celebrated of his animal poems, 'To a Mouse, on turning her up in her Nest, with the Plough, November, 1785'. Stanza 3 draws both on Burns's superb command of spoken Scots and on his memory of a religious text. 'I'll get a blessing wi' the lave,/An' never miss't' recalls a verse in the Book of Deuteronomy. A forgotten sheaf is to be left 'for the stranger, for the fatherless, and for the widow: that the Lord thy God may bless thee'. In the stanza immediately preceding this, Burns has described the mouse as his 'fellow-mortal', apologising for the rude way in which Man has broken 'Nature's social union'. To this general philosophical position, a familiar one in eighteenth-century thought, he now adds an Old Testament example. The harvest mouse from this point of view becomes 'the stranger', towards whom charity is a solemn duty. An echo of the command 'thou shalt not go again ... it shall be for the stranger' is no more than a thought in the passing – yet one which subtly adds to the meaning of what is being said.

The natural manner in which the poet addresses the mouse is the most distinctive feature of the poem. What stands out in this poem is a wryly aware tenderness towards a vulnerable little creature. 'To a Mouse' gains its effects mainly through the poet's relaxed tone; it is as if we were privileged to be with the poet as he muses to himself in the field at the time of the incident. Instead of callously dismissing as trivial what has happened, he empathises with the one rendered homeless, showing that he understands the nature of such anxiety, present alike in a mouse and in vulnerable human beings. It is an apparently simple poem which nevertheless expresses exceptional sensitivity.

Satire

Outstanding among the satirical poems which Burns published in 1786 is 'The Holy Fair'. It is a beautifully controlled mockery of the Mauchline summer communion of 1785. Behind this poem lies a long tradition of vernacular Scottish poetry describing social events. Robert Fergusson's 'Leith Races' is a deftly updated urban equivalent of a medieval 'peasant brawl' poem. Fergusson follows tradition in writing with his tongue in his cheek, yet without making the amusing scenes he describes subscribe to a controlling point of view. He introduces the presiding figure of Mirth – which was to give Burns a vital hint for 'The Holy Fair'. What distinguishes 'Leith Races' from 'The Holy Fair' is Burns's observation of a phenomenon particularly associated with the West of Scotland, namely a craze for country communions. They were breeding-grounds both of 'enthusiasm' in the eighteenth-century sense of fanatical zeal, and of uninhibited merry-making. The power of Burns's poem flows from the fact that he knows his subject at first hand, and holds to a consistent point of view. 'The Holy Fair' is full-blooded satire, turning on a contrast between professed and actual inclinations.

Its first stanza shows Burns enjoying the beauty and freshness of a calm Sunday morning, the single day when he does not have to work. In this way Burns establishes that he as narrator belongs to the world of Nature and instinctive living. He then adds to the reader's sense of anticipation by describing his meeting with 'a sweet lass', *Fun*, who immediately tells him that two miserable-looking creatures travelling beside her are *Superstition* and *Hypocrisy*, and that all three are on their way to Mauchline Holy Fair. The bond between *Fun* and Burns as narrator is one of pleasure in each other's company, and in shared 'remarkin'. That they happen to be of opposite sexes clearly adds to the poet's zestful enjoyment of the occasion. His relationship with the laughing girl is deliberately presented as the most natural thing in the world, preparing the way for our amused recognition of the place of sex in country life later in the poem. One of the main positives of 'The Holy Fair', a male–female attraction, is not at this point contained by a repressive code, although Hypocrisy is already at hand; whereas later, the effect of a life-denying social code will be to provoke a riotously carnal reaction among younger members of the community.

'The Holy Fair' gains its effects in two ways: by presenting group scenes, and by focusing on particular individuals, through a technique which seems to point forward to the twentieth-century camera's zoom lens. Burns robs one of his main targets 'The Elect' of all dignity by mentioning 'a set of lads' with no more spiritual aim than to wink at the girls as they make for chairs. Group scenes offer Burns an opportunity to introduce homely, down-to-earth humour which helps to ensure that the overall tone of the poem remains pleasantly relaxed. Incidents which he describes have the effect of emphasising sex and drink over against religiosity as primary motivating human values even in professedly holy Mauchline. In driving home his point about natural carnality prevailing over holy objectives, Burns leads the poem to its conclusion and caps the poem with a final suggestive picture.

> There's some are fou o' *love divine*
> There's some are fou o' *brandy*;
> An' monie jobs that day begin,
> May end in *Houghmagandie*
>   Some ither day.

Thus it is put beyond doubt that instinctive pleasure-seeking is an essential part of human nature, and one with more to recommend it than a life-denying and hypocritical attitude masquerading as religious purity.

'Holy Willie's Prayer' has an epigraph from Pope's 'Rape of a Lock': 'And send the godly in a pet to pray'. In August 1784 Burns's friend Gavin Hamilton was cited for his neglect of public worship before the annual communion at Mauchline – the very event which would be satirised in 'The Holy Fair'. In an 'argument' introducing 'Holy Willie's Prayer', Burns alludes to the part played by a leading Mauchline elder, William Fisher, in provoking enmity against Hamilton.

The poem is a poised and sustained dramatic monologue, of a quality to compare with any of Browning's in English in the following century.

From the beginning, Burns uses his familiarity with the idiom of Scottish religious devotion and his mastery of verse form to destroy Willie Fisher's character from within. Moreover, he makes Willie observe the ordered structure of Presbyterian prayer. Unconscious ironies abound. The monologist's confident invocation of his deity, sending 'ane to heaven and ten to h-ll', is quickly followed by a gleeful meditation on the special purpose for which he, Fisher, has been called to be

> A burning and a shining light
> To a' this place.

One of Burns's weapons is deliberate juxtaposition. No sooner has Willie congratulated himself on his role as 'ruler and example/To a' thy flock' than he begins to try to 'get round' God by referring to his pardonable weaknesses of the flesh:

> But yet – O L—d – confess I must –
> At times I'm fash'd wi' fleshly lust;
> And sometimes too, in warldly trust
>   Vile Self gets in;   ·
> But thou remembers we are dust,
>   Defil'd wi' sin. –

This theme having been broached, Willie does not hesitate to cleanse his conscience by off-loading the troublesome particulars of his most recent minor lapse; then he consoles himself further by bringing his prayer back to the generalities of moralising pious reflection. Perhaps like St Paul he has been tested by having to contend with a 'thorn in the flesh'? Here the mixture of farming language and the 'language of the saints' is particularly lethal. By the time he reaches the 'petition' section of his prayer, Willie has cleared out of the way everything which might inhibit his holy zeal against Gavin Hamilton. In naming his enemy, he gives vent to energetically personal denunciation. At this point the poem recalls both an Old Testament curse of the ungodly and an occasion when Hamilton was charged by the kirk session with causing his servant to pick potatoes on the Sabbath:

> Curse thou his basket and his store,
>   Kail and potatoes. –

Yet Willie is not so completely carried away as to forget to make a final request for his own present and future prosperity:

> That I for grace and gear may shine,
>   Excell'd by nane!

'Gear' means 'property'. Willie the hypocrite is a sensual-minded materialist. Scott accurately described 'Holy Willie's Prayer' as 'exquisitely severe'. Its special art lies in Burns's combination of comic language with an accurately directed personal attack on Willie.

The Burns Stanza

Burns is a versatile metrist, with different forms at his command, but one type of stanza stands out, the verse form in which he writes 'Poor Mailie's Elegy', 'The Vision. Duan First', 'To a Mouse', and many other poems in the Kilmarnock edition. 'Standart Habbie', or the Burns Stanza, as it came to be known after his death, takes its name from a comic elegy by the seventeenth-century Scottish poet Robert Sempill about a piper who was missed by his community after his death. Comic elegy remained the first use of the stanza, though other poets added to the possible applications of an essentially versatile form in the eighteenth century.

It is difficult to overestimate the significance of 'Standart Habbie' in the case of Burns. He found it thoroughly congenial as a medium of poetic communication, and practised it so often that skill in its use became instinctive. Byron's liberating discovery in Italy in 1817 of *ottava rima*, which made possible the writing of such satires as *Beppo* and *The Vision of Judgment*, is comparable. Both poets were enabled through the use of a particular verse form to write in a relaxed colloquial style, with a resulting gain in persuasiveness. But there is one crucial difference, in that Burns found a metre which suited him early in his career as a poet, and used 'Standart Habbie' for more than satire alone. He experimented and greatly extended the range of its applications both in his 1786 collection and subsequently.

What characterises Burns's handling of the six-line stanza above all is the aptitude he displays for catching the rhythms and tones of a speaking voice. It is no accident that his 'Address to the Deil' is in 'Standart Habbie', nor that out of seven verse-epistles in the complete original Kilmarnock edition, all but two are in the same metre. Burns is essentially a social poet wishing to share ideas with his friends, and this form is ideally suited for his literary purpose.

Two tales

In Burns's Ayrshire, a social custom which helped to shorten long winter evenings was the occasion known as a 'rocking'. A number of people who lived near one another came together in somebody's house and enjoyed a *ceilidh*, exchanging news, tales, and songs. They might also spin or do other work of the kind; in such a gathering time flew past. The occasion was a genuinely communal one, expressing the interests shared by farming folk. Burns belonged to a society which relished personality, fun and joking, and local incident. To 'ca' the crack' was to chat or gossip about people, their doings, and eccentricities. A strong taste for 'character' and a fund of anecdote and miscellaneous information existed along with a love of fiddle music and song in the community of which Burns was a member. It is easy to imagine that when neighbours met, as often as not the poet was the life and soul of the company; for not only did he have the precious gift of songwriting, he was, additionally, an expert and humorous observer of human nature, deeply versed in its most amusing local variations.

This is the essential background of most of Burns's poetry. He was above all else a natural communicator, who worked with rather than against the bias of circumstances, and when asked to speak or write could appeal directly to men and women from the same rural society as himself. That his poems reached out to a wider public beyond Ayrshire was in a sense quite accidental, and remains so. He had read widely, it is true, and could amuse himself by imitating and even surpassing the literary artifice of bookish men; and like other poets, he was ambitious for fame. But all this was secondary. Burns had most universal appeal when writing about what he knew and experienced at first hand. He drew his main creative inspiration from his own people and took as his source of ideas the living language that had been his from boyhood onwards.

Many of the poems flowed from real-life situations in which Burns had been involved, and concerned actual, identifiable individuals, even if only as a starting point or in passing. Part of the pleasure for those who first heard or read his work was to learn how he had 'taken off', in satire or celebration, persons known to themselves. However, in the process of composition, the local, particularised, real-life elements were caught up in the poet's imagination and transformed, as his two fully developed narrative poems show.

The fame of Burns's second tale 'Tam o' Shanter. A Tale' has almost entirely eclipsed that of the first, 'Death and Doctor Hornbook'. He himself stated somewhat ruefully that 'Tam o' Shanter' was his 'standard performance in the poetical line'. Traditionally this brilliant and popular poem has been discussed on its own; but 'Tam o' Shanter' appears in a new light when placed beside 'Death and Doctor Hornbook', the merits of which deserve to be better known.

As already stated, Burns loved a good story and was directly affected by country superstitions to the point of sharing their 'terrors'. He was sceptical about the nature of the experiences on which they were based but found them a fine subject for poetry. There were many tales about witches relating to the old ruined church of Alloway not far from Burns's boyhood home. One of the tales which he included in a letter of June 1790 to Francis Grose, an artist friend, is virtually a prose draft of the poem 'Tam o' Shanter'. This is an extract from that letter.

On market day in the town of Ayr, a farmer . . . had been detained by his business till by the time he reached Alloway it was the wizard hour between night and morning. Though he was terrified, with a blaze streaming from the kirk, yet as it is a well-known fact, that to turn back on these occasions is running by far the greatest risk of mischief, he prudently advanced on his road ... He was surprised and entertained to see a dance of witches merrily footing it around their old sooty blackguard master, who was keeping them alive with the power of his bagpipe.

What the prose extract does not bring out is the wonderful humour of the poem. One reason for the popularity of 'Tam o' Shanter' is that it has a dimension of humour which appeals very widely, that of sex and marriage. Like the poet, the narrator is a married man. There are references to Tam's wife waiting at home in a rage, to the secret favours of the landlady, and to Tam's longing for the witches to be 'in their teens'. Sexual comedy provides the supreme event in the tale as the unseen Tam shouts out his admiration for the youngest of the witches. The humour of physical desire transforms the atmosphere of 'Tam o' Shanter' and helps to universalise the fable.

Although 'Tam o' Shanter' is primarily a comic tale, it contains passages of apparently solemn moralising which emphasise the dangers that await Tam in his pursuit of various pleasures. The narrator expresses occasional warnings to Tam in a friendly manner in Scots as he advises Tam that he should have followed his wife's advice about drink, and also, more formally, in English when in melancholy mood he warns that pleasures like poppies are shortlived. He uses English in a turning away from the course of the poem to address whisky which he personifies as 'John Barleycorn', but immediately follows this with four lines of excellent Scots which culminate in Tam's throwing all caution to the winds and being game to take on anything and anyone. In another aside from the main sequence of the poem the omniscient narrator warns Tam in Scots of the effect the witches would have had on him if they had all been young.

What Burns achieves throughout is the skilful handling of transitions between Scots and English right up to the very last stanza with its moral, poised between the two,

Now, wha this tale o' truth shall read,
Ilk man and mother's son, take heed:
Whene'er to drink you are inclin'd,
Or cutty-sarks run in your mind,
Think, ye may buy the joys o'er dear,
Remember Tam o' Shanter's mare.

'Tam o' Shanter' and 'Death and Doctor Hornbook' are comic tales about a drunken hero who meets Something on his way home at night but 'Death and Doctor Hornbook' was composed in 1785 and 'Tam o' Shanter' not until 1790. The 1785 poem was conceived as a satire, the second as an extended illustration of the legend of Alloway Kirk. 'Death and Doctor Hornbook' is, on one level, a personal lampoon or satire on the character of the schoolmaster John Wilson or 'Jock Hornbook' who also gave medical advice and dispensed drugs – hence the 'Doctor' in the title. A hornbook was a first book for children learning to read which consisted of a leaf of paper with the alphabet or numbers or even the Lord's prayer printed on it, framed and mounted on board and protected by a sheet of transparent horn. 'Hornbook' is therefore the perfect choice of surname for a satire on a local teacher. It is also a poem, however, which mocks at the idea of Death by robbing it of terror and solemnity.

Burns creates comic and satiric effects at the expense both of Death and of Hornbook. Some of these are direct and simple in content; others depend upon a combination of coarseness and sophisticated literary irony (lines 85–90); still others, upon rapid linguistic transitions (lines 127–31). 'Tam o' Shanter' corresponds to the earlier poem in that it once again incidentally reduces the dignity of a supernatural power, this time the Devil. The two tales operate within similar limits. The most obvious technical difference between them is that 'Death and Doctor Hornbook' is a first-person narrative while 'Tam o' Shanter' is told in the third person. This difference between dramatic monologue and 'external' narrative is radical. One of the subtlest features of 'Tam o' Shanter' is that most of the action is viewed through the eyes of a 'crony narrator'. Despite this, there is a clear similarity in treatment of the subject between the poems. Fundamental to the success of each is the projection of the character of the intoxicated hero. The exhibition of his credulous personality and heightened state of consciousness is in each case the 'action' before the action proper, building up suspense and making possible both unusual narrative economy at the climax and an ironic conclusion. In other words, the hero holds the tale together, rather than events. We sympathise with the hero's moments of glory and of terror, understand what he is going through, and share his relief at the end.

Songs

Song-writing was an early interest of Burns, one which grew steadily as his life went on. He was familiar with the songs and dances of Ayrshire just as he was with the superstitions of the countryside. In his later years he became so deeply involved in the collecting, editing, and writing of songs that he made many jokes about his hobby. Burns played the fiddle and often when he heard a traditional tune for the fiddle he liked he would try and make up words which he thought would match the tune. He developed an instinctive knowledge for a good tune, coupled with an aptitude for matching words to it. Along with this basic understanding went a wish to bring together as many of the fine melodies of Scotland as he could and to supply them with appropriate words.

Especially after he had begun to collaborate with James Johnson on *The Scots Musical Museum* in 1787, he saw his role as 'Scotia's bard' increasingly in terms of song-collecting. Sometimes he travelled miles on horseback to collect traditional tunes. He thought about song in social terms, and wanted to give back to the Scottish people in the best possible form what he believed to belong to them, namely a heritage of fine tunes and accompanying words. His purpose could be described as part poetic, part musical, and part antiquarian. Fundamentally, he was obeying artistic and patriotic instinct. Some churchgoers, however, disapproved of songs and dancing and thought that they were anti-religious, but Burns held to his convictions despite opposition.

Song differs from melody as such in that it requires words and the voice for completeness. Burns believed that by adding words to melody it ought to be possible to release the full expressive potential within the tunes of his native land. Verses were needed to convey the sentiment or quality of feeling which a good tune often suggested to him, but which could be fully articulated only through a combination of melody and words. Equally, he took the view that to verse which otherwise might exist only at the level of writing, music adds a fresh dimension, and with it the exciting communicative possibility of actual performance.

Part 4

Hints for study

How to read eighteenth-century Scots poetry

Cultural background

Understanding that Scotland two hundred years ago had its own customs and outlook is essential. In the eighteenth century Scotland's system of farming began to change. Previously land was divided into strips or rigs and several families might rent a farm together but the farmers had short leases or in some cases no leases at all and were extremely poor so that they could not afford to improve what land they had. They were often facing starvation as seed did not germinate in inadequately drained and water-logged land. There were no hedges to give shelter from the strong winds and only a few stone dykes round the houses and cornyard to protect the harvested crops from the livestock. Farmers and their families also went hungry because the land was overworked or overgrazed and apart from dung they used no fertiliser partly because they did not know about the advantages of using lime but mostly because they could not afford to buy it.

Burns describes in 'The Twa Dogs. A Tale' the struggle 'poor tenant-bodies, scant o' cash' had to pay the rent to the landowner's representative known as the factor. In winter there was often not enough feed to keep all of the animals alive and a certain number were retained for breeding purposes only. When Burns was a boy his family stayed at Mount Oliphant farm for twelve years in extremely restricted circumstances – an experience Robert never forgot. They could not afford to pay for anybody to help and Robert did a man's work. Burns was a farmer first of all in Ayrshire and although he never experienced famine he and his family were almost made destitute by bad weather and poor harvests in 1784 and 1785 when he farmed with his brother Gilbert at Mossgiel.

One must remember that Burns was both a working tenant farmer and a natural rebel. The opening of 'The Vision. Duan First' and the second verse-epistle to Lapraik show just how physically demanding farming life could be. Burns's circumstances prevented him from choosing the life of a full-time writer. Instead, he had to work very long hours six days of the week. Summer holidays were unknown, as were days without tending crops and giving attention to livestock. It was partly because he objected to the economic unfairness of the society in which he lived that Burns was a rebel.

There was also, however, his objection to the unreasonable demands and restraints imposed by ecclesiastical authority. Tyranny, whether of Kirk or landlord, Burns hated; he had suffered under both, and knew their sting. Better than most of his neighbours, Burns realised that liberty – economic, religious, and political – was a 'glorious feast'. Nevertheless, he tried not to be consumed by bitterness. Only when Authority and Hypocrisy joined hands did he cease to temper his ridicule with good nature. Very characteristic are the good-humoured recognition of the fatiguing nature of life on the land in 'While new-ca'd kye [newly calved cattle] rowte[low] at the stake', and the refusal to compromise with a hypocrite supported locally by the Church of Scotland, which together make 'Holy Willie's Prayer' an assertion of the poet's personal values.

Reading Burns's poetry

This poet is a warm-hearted, sympathetic human being, who enjoys both Nature and the human companionship of friends and lovers; who does not deny his failings; who believes in and expresses in his work the simpler human virtues – honesty, friendliness, generosity, kindness to humble men and women and to the animals in the fields. But Burns is also a master of his craft. The more we read the best of his work, the more we admire his technique. The ease with which he moves in many elaborate verse patterns, adapting form to content with unerring skill; the sureness with which he selects the right word, the observant phrase; the deftness with which he weaves vowels and consonants into musical cadences and patterns – these elements of Burns's technique are sometimes overlooked; but the art is there, and in rich measure.

Almost all poetry is better understood for being read aloud. In a lot of older poetry, including that of eighteenth-century Scotland, this was its first medium anyway; poetry was there to be read or recited and to be shared in the company of others. There is no better way to gain quickly an understanding of the devices which hold a poem together – rhyme and features of rhythm – than by listening to it. Get other people to read the poem to you. If you happen to know someone who is Scottish by birth or who has lived in Scotland, by all means turn to that person first, but please bear in mind that the vital thing, as with all language learning, is to be willing to experiment.

A practical approach is to read a Burns poem to your friends and ask what they think of it, what comes into their minds when they hear it read. Reading Burns's Scots aloud may initially seem strange and you may feel that you are making mistakes; it does not matter as there is no single right or wrong way of speaking words which are no longer in daily use even in

Scotland. Treat it lightly and you are, in your own independent way, showing a sense of humour which was a principal element of Burns's philosophy of life.

A good poem has many different possible meanings, just as a good piece of music or art can be interpreted differently. Particular phrases, images, verses and lines will stand out and have special meaning when read aloud, perhaps because the Scots is complicated or even expresses a complicated idea simply. Maybe you have had to work hard at getting the meaning and then suddenly find a fresh angle on the poem or there might be a discovery of an idea about life which you have not had before but which you nevertheless consider to be valid. Sometimes phrases or ideas may relate to something you have experienced. Though the thoughts and feelings are the poet's own, you will find yourself sharing some of them. Build on what you recognise by expressing your own thoughts, to deepen your understanding of a poem. Do not be discouraged by the language difficulty.

It is hard for all readers of Burns. Even for his fellow Scots in his own lifetime Burns had to print glossaries explaining the meaning of words that were unknown or difficult and that people in a city like Edinburgh, the capital of Scotland, would not recognise. Poems are continually changing and acquire additional shades of meaning after several readings.

Organising your work

It may help to write down what you feel about a poem. This can be a brief response to begin with. You can use words like lively, complicated, difficult, even sad. Then ask yourself why the poem is sad, lively or complicated. Is it the language used? Is it the style in which the poem is written? Is it the mood that Burns creates, for example at the start of 'The Cotter's Saturday Night'? As it happens, Burns is a poet and songwriter whose moods often help to explain the nature and specific content of his poetry. He thinks very clearly about life as he knows it, but is not an intellectual or abstract philosophical thinker in what he writes. Mood and down-to-earth experience meant more to him than systematic thinking or visionary statements of the type favoured by, say, Blake or Shelley.

It matters very much that you persist when difficulties present themselves. You have every bit as much right to hold opinions about Burns's work as the next reader. It is necessary to read with care and be willing to look up words which are new to you, and this process is not likely to be completed on a first reading. Try out various possibilities, though, and there is a strong chance that you will succeed in understanding the poet's work, text by text. Ask yourself, what is the central or key idea he is expressing? Secondary parts of the meaning of any particular poem or song will probably then fall into place.

Answering questions on Burns's poetry

As you read for a second or third time, you will make a lot of notes on individual texts and the meaning of particular words. When you come to write an essay or examination answer, however, it is necessary to bear in mind the question you choose, and to avoid simply repeating everything you know about the poet or his writings. A key word is relevance. Try to make sure that you focus clearly on the question, and support your views with evidence drawn at first hand from your reading of Burns's poetry. Do not run the risk of losing your reader by causing her or him to read through a lot of information without a direct bearing on the question set. Instead, choose what is to the point by way of examples addressing the question. A question in an examination paper is exactly what it says it is: a question. It requires that you attempt to answer as you would any other, 'real life' question, as accurately and honestly as possible. Set aside some time – perhaps a quarter of the time allowed for your answer – in which you read the question with due care, grasp the points it is trying to make, and make a plan of your answer.

A sound plan will in the first place list the points you want to make, and will also include references you want to make to the poetry. It is advisable to quote directly from the poet's work, but to do so succinctly and cogently, not wordily or at length. If you have already provided enough quoted material, it is possible to supplement this with material which requires less direct quotation. For example, if you have made an idea clear by quoting from poem A, you have the option of adding that further proof is offered by poems B and C. Even better is to be able to say which lines in poems B and C are relevant.

Make sure that you let your examiner know where your answer is going. You have a duty to be a guide in that sense, showing a clear sense of how your argument is constructed. Indicate at the beginning of your answer what you intend to do and to what areas of the poet's work you will refer. This will provide evidence of clear planning, and it will also keep the question before you and so will prevent you from following red herrings. If you find yourself running out of time in a final answer, provide a brief account, in a sentence or two, of where you have got to, and recall the original question. Keep in mind that your examiner is looking for evidence of objective knowledge of the poetry, but also for the quality of your subjective response. By including comment of an individual kind, based on study of the poems, you will persuade him or her that you know the work and have thought clearly about the question.

Sample questions

(1) 'His candle is bright, but shut up in a dark lantern' (William Cowper on Burns's poetry). Discuss the linguistic challenge facing modern

readers of *Poems in Scots and English*, making particular reference to any two or three poems.

(2) 'Form is very much part of the meaning of the poem.' Discuss with reference to 'Poor Mailie's Elegy', 'To J. S*****', or 'Address to the Deil'.

(3) Discuss in detail the poetic art of 'The Holy Fair', 'The Vision. Duan First', or 'The Cotter's Saturday Night'.

(4) 'Burns is at his best as a satirist when . . .' Develop.

(5) Write a critical commentary on 'Tam o' Shanter'.

(6) Introduce and discuss a representative group of Burns's songs, commenting on the nature of Burns's achievement as songwriter and 'songsmith'.

(7) 'A social poet, and an occasional poet'. Consider the case for seeing Burns in these terms, making reference to particular poems and songs.

Sample answer

(1) 'His candle is bright, but shup up in a dark lantern' (William Cowper on Burns's poetry). Discuss the linguistic challenge facing modern readers of *Poems in Scots and English*, making particular reference to any two or three poems.

The quotation written by the English poet Cowper, who was Burns's contemporary, is at least as appropriate for Burns's poetry today as it was then. It is true that, initially, Lowland Scots has for many people the effect of a dark lantern blocking the light of the candle; it is so dense that it makes it difficult to see the true meaning of the poem on a first reading. But once the Scots words become familiar and lose their seeming impenetrability, the warmth, humour, and freshness of expression and feeling at the heart of Burns's poetry shine through to make this verse well worth discovering.

To a Louse shows just how skilfully and effectively Burns handles Scots as he addresses the louse and then Miss Jenny who is completely unaware of the louse's presence on her fashionable bonnet. Burns is in church and bored when he suddenly sees a louse crawling on the hat of a girl in the congregation who gives herself airs. He greets the surprising discovery of the louse with a triumphant 'Ha!'. This 'crowlan ferlie' is indeed a crawling wonder for daring to 'strunt' around such a grand hat on such a pretentious person. Burns addresses the louse in a familiar tone as if he is talking in Scots to a friend. 'Ha! whare ye gaun, ye crowlan ferlie! . . . I canna say but ye strunt rarely,/Owre *gawze* and *lace*'. He captures perfectly in Scots the different movements the louse makes as it grows in confidence climbing up the bonnet; its 'crowlan' and 'creepan' gives way to a 'strunt', or strut, as it dares to set its 'fit' upon 'Sae fine a lady'.

This is in contrast to the usual habitat of the louse which is a beggar's 'haffet squattle' or squat wooden 'temple'. There the louse is at home as it sprawls, creeps and 'sprattles' or scrambles. These verbs convey more successfully than their English equivalents the ungainly yet stealthy progress the louse makes as it finally gets right to the 'vera tapmost, towrin height' of the crown of the bonnet.

Nothing is safe from the predatory louse, not even the trailing ribbons of the 'fatt'rels' or loose pieces of trimmings made of gauze and lace which were added to the balloon-shaped bonnet. In the third verse there are two lines without any Scots at all. The use of English in these lines contrasts with the rest of the verse in Scots and emphasises the loneliness this louse must feel as he 'seeks his dinner' alone instead of 'in shoals and nations' and 'thick plantations' in his accustomed haunts.

Burns continues with some of his densest but most vivid language in the next two stanzas. The louse is ever bolder as he dodges in and out of the trimmings which were added to the Lunardi. In an unusual image he likens the louse's poking his nose out to a gray 'grozet' or gooseberry. To rhyme with 'grozet' he chooses another unfamiliar Scots word 'rozet' or resin. 'Fell', 'smeddum', and 'Wad dress your droddum' would not be nearly so telling if written in English. Once the language is understood and the colloquial tone is accepted the humour in the stanzas shines out. It's one thing to find a louse on an old flannel cap worn by an 'auld wife' or in the vest of a wee ragged boy 'some bit duddie boy', and another to find it on 'Miss's fine Lunardi, fye!' However the reality is that the louse is there and making itself at home. Tongue in cheek, Burns concludes the scandalised observation with the very English exclamation 'fye' which not only underlines the social difference and the distance between Miss and the louse's usual hosts but also highlights the louse's impudence and presumption in daring to consider her as a suitable target in the question which follows 'How daur ye do't?'

There is little real linguistic challenge in the next two stanzas. Burns offers Jenny simple, direct advice in the only verse in the poem which he addresses to her, and prepares us for the wish expressed in the last stanza. His words are world-famous, despite the use of Scots in lines 1, 3, and 5. Easily understood English conveys in line 2 part of the poem's moral or principal concluding idea

To see oursels as others see us,

balancing the colloquial Scots in which Burns has spoken earlier to the louse.

'Tam o' Shanter' is probably the only poem of its length in any European language which is recited, read aloud, and acted at social events held each year on or near the poet's birthday to honour his memory. It brings in a number of speakers, among them Tam, his wife Kate who scolds him, and the shapely young witch Nannie. The narrator too has a speaking voice, at times sympathetic to Tam, but at other moments less so, when the poet has apparently decided to point out the errors of Tam's ways. He has been described as a 'crony narrator' when he takes the viewpoint of the hero. At such points, Burns tends to use lots of Scots words, because Scots is the language Tam speaks himself. At the climax of the young witch's dance, for instance, he writes

> Weel done, Cutty Sark!

as these are the very words Tam would exclaim loudly in his excitement. Similarly when Kate is scolding Tam for drinking, talking and flirting she speaks down to earth Scots. Burns captures the exact idiom as Kate tells Tam first of all that he is a 'skellum' or rascal; then without stopping to catch breath she continues to give him his character as 'A blethering, blustering, drunken blellum;' who is not sober from 'November till October' and takes any excuse to get drunk to misspend time 'wi' Kirkton Jean'. Her prophecy combines English syntax with further characteristic Scots forms – 'catch'd wi' warlocks in the mirk' and 'auld haunted kirk'. English is used, on the other hand, to convey conventional moral sentiments, as in the passage beginning at line 59:

> But pleasures are like poppies spread,
> You seize the flower, its bloom is shed.

Certain Scots words and phrases recur in connection with drink – for example 'fou' which means drunk. Friends and neighbours sit 'bousing' or drinking and 'getting fou'. Tam has regularly been 'roaring fou' (line 26) according to his wife Kate, and with his 'ancient, trusty, drouthy crony' has even been 'fou for weeks thegither' (line 44). 'Drouthy' or thirsty is another recurring word. 'Nappy' and 'reaming swats, that drank divinely', ale at two pence a pint known as 'tippeny' and whisky or 'usquabae', also called 'John Barleycorn', take their toll of Tam's 'noddle'. In the moral at the end of the tale Burns uses English as he advises every

> man and mother's son, take heed;
> Whene'er to drink you are inclined
> Or cutty sarks run in your mind,
> Think, ye may buy the joys o'er dear,
> Remember Tam o' Shanter's mare.

Whereas the storyteller has been warning about the perils of drink and the fate of Tam's mare, in English, he is really thinking about the young witch and her 'cutty sark'. The Scots lantern shines clearly.

Part 5

Suggestions for further reading

Texts of the poems

LOW, DONALD (ED.): *Robert Burns: Poems in Scots and English*, Everyman Paperbacks, 1993.

McGUIRK, CAROL (ED.): *Robert Burns: Selected Poems*, Penguin Classics, 1993.

LOW, DONALD (ED.): *The Songs of Robert Burns*, Routledge, 1993. The first complete edition, including both words and music.

Burns's letters

ROY, G. ROSS (ED.): *The Letters of Robert Burns*, Oxford University Press, 1985. Exact text of all the main letters.

Biography

MACKAY, JAMES: *Burns: A Biography of Robert Burns*, Mainstream, 1992. Detailed and comprehensive.

Criticism

SIMPSON, KENNETH: *The Poetry of Robert Burns*, Aberdeen: Scotsnotes Series, ASLS, 1994. Clear and helpful.

SIMPSON, KENNETH (ED.): *Burns Now*, Edinburgh: Canongate Academic, 1994. Essays for senior students.

Reference

ROBINSON, MAIRI (ED.): *A Concise Scots Dictionary*, Aberdeen University Press, 1985. Contains a good historical indroduction.

The author of these notes

DONALD A. LOW was educated at the Universities of St Andrews and Cambridge. He returned to St Andrews as a lecturer, before moving to Stirling University, where he is now a Professor in the Department of English Studies. His many publications on Burns include *Robert Burns: Poems in Scots and English* and *The Songs of Robert Burns.*